Has Democracy Failed
Women?

Democratic Futures series

Stephen Coleman, *Can the Internet Strengthen Democracy?*
Donald F. Kettl, *Can Governments Earn Our Trust?*

Drude Dahlerup

Has Democracy Failed Women?

polity

First published in 2018 by Polity Press

Polity Press
65 Bridge Street
Cambridge CB2 1UR, UK

Polity Press
350 Main Street
Malden, MA 02148, USA

ISBN-13: 978-1-5095-1636-0
ISBN-13: 978-1-5095-1637-7(pb)

A catalogue record for this book is available from the British Library.

Typeset in 11 on 15pt Sabon
by Fakenham Prepress Solutions, Fakenham, Norfolk NR21 8NN
Printed and bound in Great Britain by Clays Ltd. St Ives PLC

The publisher has used its best endeavours to ensure that the URLs for external websites referred to in this book are correct and active at the time of going to press. However, the publisher has no responsibility for the websites and can make no guarantee that a site will remain live or that the content is or will remain appropriate.

Every effort has been made to trace all copyright holders, but if any have been inadvertently overlooked the publisher will be pleased to include any necessary credits in any subsequent reprint or edition.

For further information on Polity, visit our website:
politybooks.com

Contents

Tables and figures

Tables

Tables and figures

Figures

Preface

Has democracy failed women? Many would claim yes, since women have less than a quarter of the seats in the world's parliaments, and since the elimination of gender inequality is not a salient issue high on the political agenda almost anywhere. Most of the political leaders in the world are men. Just take a look at the usual "family" photo taken at a world summit!

However, others would stress that women, from a position of total exclusion, are now gradually being included in elected assemblies all over the world, and more and more countries have experienced having a woman prime minister or president. We now even see women as finance and defense ministers – some of the last male bastions in politics.

The UN World Conference on Women in Beijing in 1995 represented a major shift of the global discourse away from the previous focus on women's (alleged) lack of qualifications and political interest to a new focus on the lack of inclusiveness of the political institutions themselves. This is also the approach that I will adopt in this book.

"There [in Beijing, 1995] was an almost universal or palpable desire to be in power, to be in leadership, to change the terms of the relationship with the great globe; the mode of operation shifted from one of stating demands and needs to one of seeking control over the decision-making process," wrote Devaki Jain in her book *Women, Development, and the UN* (2005). But can this optimism be maintained today in a world of climate change, economic crisis, armed conflicts and Trumpism? Is the world on the right track towards full inclusion of women in political life, and can we rule out future backlashes?

Paradoxically, at the same time that *gender parity* in politics is included as a principle in most international declarations, we find no uniform position among feminists on the benefits or actual outcomes of including women in male-dominated political institutions, for instance by the adoption of quotas. It will, however, be argued in this book that old democracies as well as countries in transition to democracy need what British political scientist

Preface

Anne Phillips has called the *presence* of women, based on the new principle of parity – both as a right in itself and because women from all walks of life and from all over the world need more inclusive and well-functioning democratic political institutions to counteract the discriminatory effects of free market forces. The complexity of achieving parity in political life will be illustrated with examples from my work as an advisor on the political empowerment of women around the world.

Drude Dahlerup
Professor of Political Science
Stockholm, April 2017

Acknowledgments

I want to thank Louise Knight of Polity Press for suggesting this short book on women and democracy as a way to present an update of my many years of research on this topic and my recent experiences as a global advisor on how to empower women in political life in countries as diverse as Cambodia, Sierra Leone, China, Egypt, Tunisia, Kosovo, Bhutan, Kenya and the Ivory Coast. I am grateful to all the hard-working women's NGOs and the many elected female politicians and government ministers who have shared with me invaluable insights into the barriers women meet in politics and how to overcome them.

I thank Nana Kalandadze and Rumbidzai Kandawasvika-Nhundu, International IDEA, and Zeina Hilal, the Inter-Parliamentary Union, for our great collaboration around the Global Quota

Acknowledgments

Website, www.quotaproject.org. I also want to thank all my wonderful new friends in the Global Civil Society Advisory Group (2012–15) to UN Women's Executive Director, first to Michelle Bachelet, followed by Phumzile Mlambo-Ngcuka.

Emil Johansson, Alma Jonssen and Vaselis Petrogiannis have worked as research assistants with the coding of the Gender Quota Database (GQD), Stockholm University, 2014, and Tova Ask has worked as research assistant on various tables in the book. The DanishVelux Foundations have contributed through their financial support for the GRIP research project, based at Aalborg University, Denmark.

I am grateful to my colleagues at the department of Political Science at Stockholm University, especially Lenita Freidenvall and Diane Sainsbury, and to my extended research network all over the world for discussions on the development of Gender & Politics as a research field. Finally, I am grateful to my Danish-Swedish-Spanish family for so much in life, and I want to dedicate this book to my marvelous grandchildren, Carlos 8, Otto 6, Silas 5 and Alva 2.

1

Exclusion Without Words

As the daughter of a feminist mother, I knew that my high-school teacher was wrong when, without any reservations, he taught us that the ancient city-state of Athens was the "cradle of democracy." Can one really speak of democracy when a large portion of the population, perhaps even the majority, is excluded from political decision-making, as was the case in ancient Greece for women as well as for immigrants, slaves and workers? As a schoolgirl I protested in class, though to no avail.

The feminist critique of the celebration of the city-state of Athens as the cradle of democracy focuses on what we might call the "who" of democracy, that is, those who are included in, and those groups which are excluded from, political decision-making. This perspective challenges the traditional discourse, be it in political theory or in actual political life, which gives priority to the procedures – the "how" of democratic decision-making. Can one honestly speak of democracy if women and minorities are excluded, even if the procedures followed among the privileged men in the polity fulfill all the noble criteria of fair elections, deliberation and rotation of positions? In general, it is necessary to challenge the traditional definitions of democracy.

From a feminist perspective, the full and equal inclusion of women in politics is important as a right in itself because of the visible and highly symbolic value of political representation. Moreover, women's movements have argued that the inclusion of women is necessary in order to change the political agenda and the political decisions. To those who say that the gender of politicians does not matter, feminists would respond: imagine a parliament or government with 80 percent women – would that not immediately cause a masculine uproar?

Two further dimensions of democracy are relevant here. The feminist critique also maintains that (although this is contested) there is a connection between those who participate in the decision-making and the policy result, that is, between women's numerical representation and what we, thirdly, might call the "what" of democracy; in other words, which issues reach the political agenda and whose interests are being paid attention to? Some researchers talk further about the "where" of democracy as a fourth dimension.[1] Democratic decision-making can be an ideal throughout society, from the kitchen table, the bedroom and the workplace, to education, sport and in civil society at large. Openness and inclusion in decision-making wherever it may take place are no doubt crucial for what happens within formal political institutions, and vice versa. The primary focus of this book is on the elected assemblies, the political parties, the governments and other key political institutions, including the pressure put on these institutions by national and transnational women's movements and feminist scholarship.

Plan of the book

An ambiguous relationship exists between women and democracy. This relationship will be analyzed from a historical neo-institutionalist perspective, with its focus on the inertia, also called the "stickiness," of institutions, many of which were formed before women had the right to participate. This approach implies a focus on formal as well as informal norms, including studies of the ways in which women's under-representation is discussed (the discursive framework), and the constant pressure put on political parties and governments by women's movements. This is all analyzed from a feminist scholarly perspective, stressing the unequal power relations between women and men.

Chapter 1 analyzes the early discussions about women's right to vote before and just after the First World War. Key concepts to be used in this book are introduced, and references are made to contemporary discussions of women in political life. Chapter 2 looks at the gradual but still incomplete inclusion of women as political representatives into elected assemblies. Chapter 3 gives an overview based on new data on the unexpected global spread of gender quotas in politics in all types of political regimes. While Chapters 2 and 3 focus on the *descriptive* representation of women (the numbers), Chapter 4 discusses the *substantive* (the policy content) and *symbolic* representation of women, including the role of the few women in leadership positions. The fifth, and final, chapter takes us to the global arena, analyzing the presence – or lack of presence – of women and gender perspectives in global governance organizations, with examples from economic governance and from women in peace-building. This chapter also presents the final conclusions of the book.

Early exclusion

For a very long time, the exclusion of women was simply a non-issue. George H. Sabine, who wrote *A History of Political Theory*, the classic textbook read by so many generations of university students, including me, discusses the exclusion of workers, slaves and foreigners from political decision-making in the city-state of Athens and finds it explicable. Yet there is not a single word about the exclusion of women!

With the adoption of the first free constitutions of the eighteenth and nineteenth centuries, which included some limited voting rights for men, it usually went without saying that women were denied such rights. The dominant perception was that the exclusion of women, and of other groups such as servants or people receiving poverty relief, from the political arena was insignificant or simply "natural." Women's right to vote and to stand for election was unimaginable far into the nineteenth century, even for the majority of women. In the

United Kingdom, it was not until the Reform Act of 1832 that voting rights became specified as a right for "male persons."[2]

Consequently, it was extremely burdensome to challenge the exclusion of women, as illustrated in the story behind the following Danish suffragist poster from 1909 about national ("political") female suffrage:

> "There is NO UNIVERSAL suffrage . . . when *women* are deprived of POLITICAL SUFFRAGE."

Today, this statement would seem self-evident, but this was not the case at the time. The old protocol tells that the Danish Women's Society, the feminist organization behind the poster, was reluctant to publish it. They feared the text would seem inappropriate and lead to protests, especially as every child learned in school that "universal suffrage" had been introduced decades before with the adoption of limited male suffrage.[3]

One might ask whether exclusion from voting rights on account of sex, race or ethnicity was not quite different in nature from the restrictions on property, income, paying taxes, being a convict or a recipient of poverty relief, or, of course, age. The latter characteristics could, at least in principle, change during one's lifetime, whereas exclusion on account of sex, race or ethnicity was for life.

The unhappy marriage between women and liberalism

Political theorist Carole Pateman has argued that the division between the public and the private spheres and the exclusion of women from the public sphere was no coincidence but rather a constitutive element when liberal democracies were first established in the nineteenth century. The public sphere was the realm of men, while the private sphere, which should be protected from intervention on the part of the government, was the proper place for women, although with the husband as the head of the household.[4]

However, the classic liberal (as well as the contemporary neo-liberal) quests for limits to the scope of government vis-à-vis the private sphere were never part of feminist ideology. Instead of liberal demands for the protection of the family from state intervention, feminists from all political camps have called on the state to recognize women's rights, and to intervene for economic redistribution and for the protection of women against domestic violence and abuse, as summed up in the familiar slogan of the

Women's Liberation Movement in the 1970s: "The private is political!"

Is the public–private division still a barrier for women in politics, even if so much has changed for women in public life all over the world? The many incidents of sexual harassment against young women during the recent Arab Uprisings, as seen for instance in the demonstrations in Tahrir Square in Egypt, should be interpreted as attacks on women's right to be in the public sphere. In the same way, the recent outbursts of sexist hate speech against female politicians on the Internet have made many women abstain from political involvement.

How could women be tacitly excluded from the right to vote in the eighteenth and nineteenth centuries when male suffrage was on the public agenda? Early liberal writer James Mill argued that a husband could represent the interests of his wife and the entire household, a view to which his son, John Stuart Mill, so eloquently objected in his seminal book *The Subjection of Women* (1869), which was immediately translated into many other languages. In 1866, J. S. Mill presented the first proposal on women's suffrage to the British parliament. Mill's vision was not *equality of result*, but what we may call "competitive equality," that is, *equality of opportunity*. The following quote is typical of his disarming logic: ". . . if the political system of the country is such as to exclude unfit men, it will equally exclude unfit women: while if it is not, there is no additional evil in the fact that the unfit persons whom it admits may be either women or men" (*The Subjection of Women*, 1869).

Looking back on attitudes towards women in the emerging liberal "democracies," it is reasonable to state that the "unhappy marriage between feminism and Marxism," expressed by American feminist scholar Heidi Hartmann,[5] was preceded by an even closer, but no less unhappy, marriage between *liberalism and feminism*. Yet the early feminists did not turn against liberalism, but instead found their main argument in the *individualism* embedded in liberalism when they argued that women are also individuals with a right to full social, economic and political citizenship. Eventually, prominent liberal leaders became among those most supportive of women's suffrage. The British Liberal Party, however, was an exception, as the liberal prime minister H. H. Asquith (1908–16), for long continued to oppose women's suffrage, which probably contributed to the militancy of the Suffragettes, as depicted so brilliantly in the film *Suffragette* in 2015.

Women's dependency, not least the humiliating position of married women, who were economically dependent on their husbands, minors in the eyes of the law, and who often did not even legally share the custody of their children, contributed to making *independence* as well as *individualism* so essential to the feminist creed, even among socialist feminists.

The Suffrage movements[6]

The history of the suffrage movements makes fascinating reading, and new research is constantly emerging. Early feminists were engaged in fighting for women's access to education and work, married women's legal status and the working conditions of female workers, but many were still reluctant to demand suffrage. The famous Seneca Falls Convention, held in upstate New York in 1848, was an exception. After a heated debate, the famous *Declaration of Sentiments and Resolutions*, which included a demand for women's franchise, was adopted, although only signed by a third of those attending, and some of those who signed even rescinded their signatures after they had returned home.

Gender, class and race
Since women in general were excluded on account of being women, one might perhaps have expected

women's suffrage to be a cause that united all women. At the beginning of the twentieth century, suffrage certainly did mobilize an extraordinarily broad range of women's organizations and even some men's groups, but the movement was split because of ideological and strategic differences. However, the *sequence* of enfranchisement of different groups – which groups got the vote first? – seems to have been crucial for the opportunity to build coalitions across class and race divisions, as the following examples illustrate.

Discussions in the United States over the 14th and 15th Amendments, which would give voting rights to freed male slaves, but not to women, led to a split over strategy within both the suffrage movement and the anti-slavery movement. In Europe, the first proposals to introduce local suffrage for women "on equal terms with men" caused conflict among suffrage advocates. Should less privileged women fight for the voting rights of unmarried women or widows who paid taxes or held property like men in order to crack the gender code? Emmeline Pankhurst and her Women's Social and Political Union (WSPU) were supportive, while Clara Zetkin, the influential leader of the German and the international socialist women's movements, declined, arguing that such a *Damenwahlrecht* (Ladies' Vote) would only serve to strengthen the propertied classes.[7]

Not an "identity" movement

Throughout this book, I argue that it is a mistake to assume some pre-existing common identity, even if women were excluded on account of their sex, and even if the opponents of women's suffrage did try to put women into one overall category with their talk of "Woman" – who by her very nature was unsuited to politics. Without any knowledge of the modern discussion about intersectionality, the suffrage activists knew very well that getting women to join their movement would require hard work and a great deal of persuasion and organization. I argue here that the feminist movement – like most other social movements – is a *political movement*, and not just what today is called an *identity movement* – and this was the case one hundred years ago as well as being true today. The consequence is not, however, that there are no common women's causes, but that they have to be constructed through debate and organizational effort. In spite of many organizational splits, suffrage was such a common issue.

The arguments

The main arguments for and against women's suffrage are analyzed below. An interesting question is to what extent any of these arguments can still be heard today.

Opponents of women's suffrage

Even if the context varied, the arguments against the enfranchisement of women were remarkably similar in all old democracies. It was argued that God or Nature had predestined women's place to be in the home (while the phrase "public women" tended to refer to prostitutes). Further, women could not be considered independent individuals, and the husband would represent the interests of the woman and of his entire household. Opponents were also worried about damaging effects: women's suffrage could destroy the family and ultimately the emerging democratic political order (as would universal suffrage for men). Women were not competent to be involved in political life; they were inexperienced and did not understand the complexity of politics; they preferred intrigues to lofty discussions of political principles. Do all these arguments belong in the past? Not entirely.

Egypt, January 2013. Our delegation of experts from the Inter-Parliamentary Union (IPU) had the opportunity to discuss over two intense hours the position of women in politics and the possibility of gender quota regulations with the almost totally male-dominated Egyptian Senate (the Shura Council). This took place during a highly turbulent period in Egypt's recent history. The National Council of Women was also present to defend their quota proposal after the (for women) disastrous first election since President Mubarak was ousted in 2011. The Salafists, like all religious fundamentalists, repeated over and over again that a woman's place is in the home. The MPs from the Muslim Brotherhood, and even many of the secular MPs, talked about the importance of being elected on the basis of merit, arguing that most women lack the qualifications for politics. Most of the senators were themselves newcomers to national politics because of the Muslim Brotherhood's landslide election in 2011. It was tempting, but would have been impolite, to ask about the Senators' own qualifications!

The argument that women lack competence and qualifications seems to pop up everywhere and certainly every time women enter new arenas or new affirmative measures are proposed, most recently in the quota debate.

The arguments of the suffrage movements
Empirical studies of the actual arguments used by the suffrage movements in various countries

around the end of the nineteenth century and beginning of the twentieth have pointed to three types of arguments in particular.[8] The first, the *rights argument*, was written into the preamble of the Declaration of Sentiments, adopted at the Seneca Falls Convention: "We hold these truths to be self-evident: that all men and women are created equal; that they are endowed by their Creator with certain inalienable rights; that among these are life, liberty, and the pursuit of happiness."

This was formulated after the United States Declaration of Independence of 1776, which stated: "All men are created equal" – but now it included women. It was based on contemporary ideas of the Law of Nature and was a powerful answer to the opponents' major point on the predestination of women by Nature or God. Some American feminists even engaged in reinterpretation of the Bible, just as feminist Muslim women in the present day work on reinterpreting the Qur'an. The rights argument sees suffrage as a symbol of full citizenship, and implies that achieving voting rights for women was fought for as a goal in itself. Consequently, there is no need to argue about what suffrage, once obtained, should be used for.

The second argument was based on the idea that women have different experiences from men and that *women's experiences* ought to be heard in political life. It is argued that the experiences of motherhood can provide an invaluable contribution to politics – a *maternalistic* perspective. Thus suffrage is seen as a means by which to change public policy. American historian Aileen Kraditor has labeled this the *expediency* argument, since the idea was that women should improve, even "purify," public life.

Thirdly, the *conflict argument* derived from the position that there are certain conflicts of interest between women and men, and that as a consequence men cannot represent women. The biased marriage laws were often mentioned, for example Title VII, Chapter 3 on illegitimate children, in the French Civil Code (*Code Napoléon*), dating from 1803, which stated: "Scrutiny as to paternity is forbidden . . . Scrutiny as to maternity is admissible"! Even if this conflict argument appears to be a logical response to the counter-argument that women have no interests of their own, it was not used as often as the first two arguments. After all, it was only men who were legally entitled to participate in the decision in parliaments and in governments to grant women the vote.

It is remarkable that all three arguments are still used today by those campaigning for having more women in politics or for *parity*, that is, full equality between women and men in political life. The rights argument is mostly referred to today as the *justice argument*: women constitute half the population, and consequently should have half the seats in elected assemblies – period! The *experience* argument is also used frequently. Radical feminists today have no reluctance about using the *conflict* argument, although, as previously, it may collide with the powerful public discourse, also found in contemporary society, that men and women have common interests and that feminists should not incite "war" between men and women. Feminists argue that the desire for harmony between women and men in private relations seems to be transferred, *ad absurdum*, to political conflicts.

Today, at least two additional arguments are used globally in claims for the equal representation of women and men. The *democracy argument*, the fourth argument, was included in the famous Beijing Platform for Action of 1995. While the first three arguments were about how political representation can help women, the democracy argument implies that only the full inclusion of women will make democracy real, and that gender parity signifies that a country is modern and democratic. "Achieving the goal of equal participation of women and men in decision-making will provide a balance that more accurately reflects the composition of society and is needed in order to strengthen democracy and promote its proper functioning" (Platform for Action, Article 181).

The argument referred to above that women's suffrage could serve to "purify" public life represented the same intention, but was hardly likely to be accepted by male political elites a hundred years ago. In contrast, the Beijing Declaration was signed by most governments of the world at the Fourth UN World Conference on Women in 1995.

The neo-liberal trend in contemporary world politics brought with it a fifth argument for the full inclusion of women – the *utility* argument – which features prominently in recent discussions about the low number of women on company boards. It is a waste not to use all talents in society, it is argued, and the inclusion of women is arguably beneficial for the company. Some advocates even maintain that the economic results of companies with many women on the board tend to be better than those of firms with fewer women, even if researchers do not agree on the direction of causality.

This utility argument conflicts with the justice argument, however, since what will happen if the inclusion of women does not improve the functioning and results of the company? In contrast, the call for gender parity, based on a pure justice argument, does not depend on "women making a difference." In general, a focus on the *exclusion of women* provides an opening for coalitions across various social cleavages and different political ideologies, since potential disagreements about how to use the new positions may be postponed to the future, an argument we will meet later in the quota debate.

Three waves of women's suffrage

Local voting rights were usually the first rights to be won by women in the period prior to the First World War, including the right to vote and stand for election to various social boards and parish councils. The local level was less controversial than national or "political" elections, and the debates reveal that these areas were considered appropriate for womenfolk to participate in. The *first wave* of granting women national suffrage came at the end of the nineteenth century and the first decades of the twentieth, including the years immediately after the end of the First World War: New Zealand was the first (1893, granting only voting rights), followed by Australia (1902, but only white women), then the

Nordic countries (1906–21), Russia (1917), Poland (1918), the United Kingdom (1918, but with a higher voting age than that of male voters until 1928), Czechoslovakia (1920) and the United States (1920). Thus many countries have been celebrating their centenaries in the last few years. Recently, Norway has argued that it was in fact the first independent country to give women the right to vote (1913), since at the time of women's suffrage New Zealand, Australia and Finland (1906) were under foreign rule.

The *second wave* of women's suffrage came around the time of the Second World War and included France, Italy, Argentina and Chile, all predominantly Catholic countries. The *third wave* was the simultaneous granting of suffrage to women and men following the decolonization and independence of many countries in the 1960s, for instance Nigeria, Rwanda, Congo and Kenya. Lastly, political assemblies without much power, and not based on free elections, have finally been opened to women on the Arab peninsula.

Defining democracy

In the end, it is a question of definition whether we choose to speak of a democratic order, even if women and minorities are excluded from the right to vote and to stand for election. But times have changed since the days of George H. Sabine's widely used textbook *A History of Political Theory*, which managed to avoid mentioning women or the position of women at all in its entire 948 pages. In his lengthy analysis of John Stuart Mill's thinking, Sabine even failed to mention, let alone to analyze, Mill's *The Subjection of Women*.[9] Male suffrage was for long considered sufficient for fulfilling the criteria of popular participation embedded in most definitions of democracy. This may explain why there were no boycotts of Switzerland, which did not grant women the right to vote at the federal level until 1971.

Today, all academics view universal suffrage for both women and men of all races and classes as one of the defining criteria for declaring a country to be democratic – in principle at least. Yet, American sociologist Pamela Paxton has revealed some amazing discrepancies in the works of well-known scholars between the researchers' initial definition of democracy, which always includes real universal suffrage, and their actual dating of when a country became a democracy, with a maximum difference of 123 years (Switzerland).[10] Did France become a democracy in the middle of the nineteenth century or only after women obtained suffrage, as late as 1944? The United Kingdom – usually labeled the cradle of parliamentary democracy – is often called a democracy from 1918, even if women did not get the right to vote at the same age as men until 1928. Many researchers date the status of the United States as a democracy to 1870 – rather than to 1920 or to the electoral reforms of the 1960s and 1970, which aimed to secure *de facto* voting rights for black people. Such discrepancies have major implications for investigations into the factors leading to the emergence of democracy.

A gender perspective on the transition to democracy

Should women be seen as laggards in the development of democracy? We now move from the more conceptual discussions to look at newer research into the factors that facilitate transition to democracy. Rather than viewing democracy in terms of a dichotomy, as an either/or, it is more fruitful for this discussion to talk about degrees of democracy or different levels of the quality of democracy, as is done in various indexes of democracy, such as the Freedom House's Index and *The Economist* Intelligence Unit's Democracy Index (https://freedomhouse. org/report/freedom-world, www.systemicpeace.org/

polity/polity4.htm, https://infographics.economist.com/2017/DemocracyIndex).

In previous research, socio-economic growth, cultural modernization and institutional development, and perhaps additionally political will, have been considered to be the main determinants of democratic development. In terms of the sequence of events, T. H. Marshall wrote in his classic analysis of citizenship that civil rights came first, followed by political rights and lastly social rights. Feminist scholars have, however, disparaged this analysis for being modeled on white men. In her book *Engendering Transitions* (Oxford University Press, 2007), British political scientist Georgina Waylen criticized the gender blindness of contemporary research and started a whole wave of feminist literature on models of transitions to democracy from a gender perspective.

The most recent *Varieties of Democracy* (*V-Dem*) project turns on its head the argument of women as laggards in this respect, thereby also criticizing previous research on transitions to democracy for its gender blindness. Through a sequence analysis covering 160 countries over the period 1900–2012, the *V-Dem* project shows that political liberalization tends to precede democratization and that liberal rights for both women and men strengthen civil society organizations, including women's movements, which then leads on to electoral democracy. Their conclusion is: "No Democratic Transition Without Women's Rights."[11]

The *V-Dem* project makes the case that transition from autocracy to democracy occurs when the *cost of repression* becomes too high for the ruling (male) elites. This is an interesting theory, but are the costs of repression really the same for denying working-class men the vote and for excluding all women? With the exception of the suffragettes, feminist movements do not tend to resort to collective violence to obtain their goals. So it remains an open question why male political elites give in to feminist claims.

Index of democracy

A basic contemporary definition of democracy includes the following elements: (1) free, equal and fair elections based on universal suffrage; (2) transparent and accountable political institutions with low levels of corruption; (3) independent judiciary and the rule of law; (4) freedom of speech and assembly and freedom of the press; and (5) minority rights. Participation, competition and civil liberties are thus key indicators of democracy, and are also used by various contemporary indexes that rank the countries of the world according to their level of democracy.

A critical look at the most commonly used indexes of levels of democracy reveals that, apart from universal voting rights, the participation of women in politics is rarely used as an indicator of the level of democracy: among the sixty questions used by *The Economist* Intelligence Unit's Democracy Index, only one deals with women (no. 29 – on the number of women in parliament). The *Polity IV* index includes both formal and descriptive representation of women in legislatures and governments, while the Freedom House index has no indicators of women's representation under "Political Rights," but includes "equal opportunities for all, including women and minorities" under "Civil Liberties."

Conclusion

For more than a century, women's movements have challenged the traditional perception that one can still speak about democracy even if only men – or only a minority of men – are granted voting rights. A hundred years after the publication in 1909 of the poster declaring, "There is no universal suffrage, when women are deprived of political suffrage," the truth of this slogan seems self-evident. Today, universal suffrage means suffrage for both women and men, at least in theory.

After a century of struggle, the principle of "One Man – One Vote" was finally changed into "One Person – One Vote." Yet it needs to be challenged again because of the inability of many modern nation states to incorporate all of its residents, not least immigrants, into national political decision-making, even if local voting rights are often granted. At the same time, some well-established dual-nationality citizens have acquired double voting rights.

This chapter has analyzed the arguments for and against women's suffrage. In the end, it was the suffragists who won. However, a more structural perspective on the adoption of women's right to vote and to stand for election highlights the significant changes in the position of women in society as a consequence of the general socio-economic transformations during the early days of capitalism. Cultural changes have also played a significant role, and, especially, religious conflicts seem to have postponed women's right to vote and stand for election, according to newer research.

Winning the right to vote was no doubt a significant breakthrough for women as citizens. There are numerious narratives of women who proudly went to polling stations for the first time. There was a relatively high turnout among women from the very start, and they soon used their voting rights to the same extent as men – today, sometimes even more so. However, global suffrage for women did not ensure that democracy stopped failing women, as the following chapters will show.

2

Breaking Male Dominance in Politics

Women occupy fewer than a quarter of the seats in the world's parliaments and are grossly under-represented among the world's political leaders. The political representation of women is a good test of a country's claim to democracy, argues British political scientist Joni Lovenduski. It is "a fundamental feminist concern, although its impor-tance has not always been acknowledged."[1] While real universal suffrage today is seen as a defining criterion of democracy, the continuous under-representation of women might not be labeled undemocratic, but male dominance, without doubt indicates a *democratic deficit*.

Why does it take such a long time to achieve equality between women and men in political life? To answer this question we have to understand the mechanisms of exclusion and inclusion, and examine what is known in political science as "the secret garden of politics," that is, the process of selection and nomination of candidates for election.

The theme of this chapter is the presence of women in elected assemblies, also called "descriptive representation" (referring to the numbers of women), as opposed to the "substantive representation" of women (the policy content), which will be discussed later. One would assume that women's representation in democratic countries would exceed the level found in semi- or non-democratic states. However, as this chapter shows, new "fast track" models of development in the Global South are challenging the inertia of the "old" democracies.

Women as intruders

The right to vote and the right to stand for election are usually treated as a single package, since historically these rights have, with a few exceptions, been obtained simultaneously. However, they are not identical issues. The resistance to women entering elected assemblies has been much fiercer than opposition to granting them voting rights, since their access to positions as elected representatives relates directly to the distribution of power in society and challenges the traditional political elites.

The first female politicians were literally *intruders* into male spaces. "Can we not smoke in Parliament any longer," early twentieth-century male MPs asked anxiously. The bars in the UK Houses of Parliament remained men-only for a long time, and a special Women's Room was established at the Palace of Westminster, as in several other parliaments, after women MPs were admitted. Winston Churchill vividly expressed his sense of women as intruders, as Lady Astor recalled, when she had complained that the male MPs did not speak to her at all: "I remember Winston Churchill, you see . . . He said to me once: 'We hoped to freeze you out,' and then he added: 'When you entered the House of Commons, I felt like a woman had entered my bathroom and I had nothing to protect myself with, except a sponge.'"[2] This quotation shows the cultural inertia – or what in neo-institutionalist theory is called the "stickiness" – of the political institutions, which were established before women had the right to enter. Male dominance is much more than just a numerical majority.

What constitutes male dominance in politics?

Let us begin this analysis of the under-representation of women by defining some terms more precisely. Today one hears people talking already about "gender equality," when women have reached 30 percent and men 70 percent – or even about "female dominance" when the share of women approaches 30–40 percent.

According to the categories in Table 2.1, the term "male monopoly" should only be used when referring to a situation in which there are mostly

Table 2.1. Degrees of male dominance based on numerical representation of women

Degree	Percentage of women elected
Male monopoly	< 10
Small minority of women	10–25
Large minority of women	25–40
Gender balance	40–60

Note: In statistical terms, the four degrees are defined as: < 10% women; 10–24.99% women; 25–39.99% women; and 40–60% women and men. The intervals used in the table follow the actual historical development of women's representation, with a very long period of fewer than 10 percent women MPs. Degrees of female dominance can be defined in the same way, but reversed.

men, with women making up less than 10 percent. Conversely, a female monopoly means a proportion of women of 90 percent or more. This means that we should not refer to "55–59 percent women" among students of law or medicine as cases of "female dominance," as it is sometimes described, but as cases of "gender balance." Meanwhile, the feminist critique of political institutions is much broader in scope than a mere examination of women's numerical under-representation. Moreover, we have to move beyond formal suffrage and into a study of the informal norms and practices of the political institutions.

Consequently, we will now dig deeper into how democracies, as well as other regimes, fail women. Table 2.2 presents six areas of male dominance, with the numerical dimension listed first. Politics as a workplace, with its written and unwritten rules, forms the second area in which male dominance is to be found. Today, female politicians all over the world complain that inequalities seem to be embedded in the walls of their workplace: from the harsh tone in political debates to exclusion from informal meetings and problems with family obligations when meetings last long into the night, etc. In the British House of Commons, the cross-party All Party Parliamentary Group (APPG) for

Table 2.2. Six dimensions of male dominance in politics

1. Representation:	Women's numerical under-representation in elected assemblies
2. Politics as a workplace:	Male-coded norms and practices in elected assemblies
3. Vertical gender segregation:	Unequal gender distribution of positions in political hierarchies
4. Horizontal gender segregation:	Limited access for women to a range of portfolios and committees
5. Public policy:	Policies biased in favor of men. Limited concern for gender equality
6. Discourses and framing:	Gendered perceptions of politicians and of gender equality policies

Source: Dahlerup and Leyenaar (2013), "Introduction," in Drude Dahlerup and Monique Leyenaar (eds), *Breaking Male Dominance in Old Democracies*, Oxford University Press, p. 8.

Women in Parliament issued a report in 2014 recommending a "zero tolerance response to unprofessional behaviour in the Chamber," referring to sexist comments from male MPs.

Another example of male dominance is where women have limited access to positions of power within parliaments and municipal assemblies, such as committee chair, leader of party group or speaker: this is vertical gender segregation, the third dimension. Is Robert Putman's "law of increasing disproportion" still valid, in the sense of "the higher up, the fewer," with regard to women? To what extent is the *glass ceiling*, a metaphor for this "iron law," being broken? The fourth dimension, horizontal gender segregation, points to the traditional division between men and women in committee work and portfolios, even in governments. We all know that there are many female ministers of social affairs. We will discuss later why we continue to label social policies "soft" issues.

The fifth dimension refers to policy-making. Which issues reach the political agenda and which are excluded? To what extent can public policy still be interpreted as biased in favor of men or groups of men, as was so unmistakably the case when the French Civil Code forbade the search for the father of a child born out of wedlock? Two questions are debated all over the world today. First, why do democracies – and in fact all political regimes – fail to protect women from sexual assaults, crimes which severely restrict women's citizenship rights? And second, why are anti-discrimination regulations still so relatively ineffective that women are still paid less on the labor market than men?

The sixth dimension concerns the gendered perceptions of politicians, especially how women politicians are depicted in the media, and how party leaders – when looking for candidates – tend to frame women within a traditional discourse of what a "strong" politician looks like. The greatest obstacle to change is the conception that the existing political structures are the natural order of things. This was especially relevant in the first decades after women's suffrage was won.

A slow start

The first elections after women's enfranchisement were a disappointment to all of those who had fought so hard for women's suffrage. Table 2.3 shows the quite different trajectories for six selected countries: all with an unbroken democratic political system since women's enfranchisement and all from the first wave of women's suffrage before or just after the First World War.

The perspective adopted in this table originates from Norwegian political scientist Stein Rokkan's studies of the processes of nation-building and democratization through thresholds gradually overcome. Table 2.3 reveals that, for the forerunners, Sweden and Denmark, it took thirty-two and forty-eight years, respectively, to pass the 10 percent

Table 2.3. Overcoming thresholds. Trajectories of women's parliamentary representation in six old democracies since suffrage

	Australia Fed [a)]	UK[b)]	Netherlands[c)]	Denmark	USA Fed[d)]	Sweden
First election with universal franchise (percent)	1903: 0[e)]	1918: 0.1 1928: 2	1918: 1 1922: 7	1918: 3	1921: 0.6	1921: 2
First election ≥10%	1996	1997	1977	1966	1993	1953
First election ≥25%	2001	2015	1994	1984	–	1979
First election ≥40%	–	–	2010	–	–	1994
Latest election (percent)	2016: 28	2015: 29	2012: 37	2015: 37	2014: 19	2014: 43

Source: Election-day figures for single or lower chamber (no rounding off).
Notes:

a) Voting rights were not universal in Australia from 1902, since Aboriginals did not gain the right to vote until the 1960s.

b) In the UK from 1918 to 1928 only women over a certain age could vote. From 1928 the voting age became identical for men and women. In 1918 Constance Markievicz was elected, but did not take up her seat.

c) In the Netherlands, women got the right to stand for election in 1918, but did not gain voting rights until 1922.

d) Jeanette Rankin was elected to the House of Representatives in 1917 from Montana, a women's suffrage state. By the 19th Amendment in 1920 voting rights were extended to all women in the USA.

e) The first woman was not elected until 1943.

threshold (i.e. numbers of women representatives in parliament); for the Netherlands it took around sixty years; it took over seventy years for the United States and the United Kingdom, and as many as ninety years for Australia – all three countries with majoritarian electoral systems. In Australia, the first woman was not elected to the House of Representatives until 1943.

Table 2.3 illustrates the inertia of the old democracies. For all the countries in Table 2.3, it took many more years and more elections to reach 10 percent than it did to go from 10 to 25 percent, indicating that stronger barriers had to be overcome in this early period. The 25 percent threshold has only recently been passed by the latecomers, with the USA still lagging behind. Only two of these six countries – the Netherlands and Sweden – have ever passed the 40 percent barrier, thereby reaching parity (40–60 percent). The threshold perspective should not be seen as a story of historical barriers that will always successively and invariably be overcome. Denmark, the Netherlands and Sweden have all recently experienced drops, and the latest election shown in Table 2.3 does not represent their highest figures, which have been 39, 41 and 47 percent women, respectively.

Recent global increase

The past two decades have seen a remarkable increase globally in women's representation in elected assemblies: from 11 percent in 1997 to 23 percent in 2017 (see Figure 2.1). The new UN discourse about the importance of the full inclusion of women in political decision-making spurred this development, pushed by the women's movements, both those working inside political institutions and the radical grass-roots feminist movements. Today, only thirty-five countries have fewer than 10 percent women as opposed to 109 twenty years earlier. This overall increase implies that women's representation is about to move from the category *small minority* (10–25 percent) to *large minority* (25–40 percent). Even so, a certain stagnation has occurred recently. While 2013 witnessed a significant gain of 1.5 percent in the world average, the increase in 2015 was only 0.5 percent.

Figure 2.1 shows an increase in all regions of the world, indicating a worldwide push for more women in politics, yet with considerable regional variations. Europe and the Americas have continuously been at the top, but today, in 2017 the Americas score the highest, first and foremost thanks to a remarkable growth in the number of

Figure 2.1. Percentage of women in parliament 1997–2017, worldwide and by region

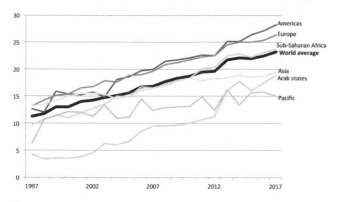

Source: www.ipu.org.

women in Latin American parliaments. In spite of large intra-regional differences, the Arab region shows a remarkable increase and has now been replaced at the bottom of the regional list by the Pacific area.

The regional perspective is important, since *international* and especially *regional competition* have proved to be effective mechanisms promoting the increased representation of women. Some researchers have called it the *contagion effect*.[3] However, for me, this sounds more like a disease spreading by itself than the effect of competition between parties or states to have the highest representation of women – all pushed by women's rights activists playing the comparative card.

The recent increase has been supported by a stronger *international discourse* on the importance of including women in political decision-making. The UN Beijing Declaration of 1995 was very influential and has been used by women's movements all over the world, as it changed the discourse on the under-representation of women from a focus on their lack of qualifications or political interest into a discussion about the "discriminatory attitudes and practices" of the political institutions themselves. The goal was now being described, not just as increasing women's representation, but as "equal participation" and "equitable distribution of power in decision-making at all levels." At the same time, however, the Declaration also speaks, in a somewhat contradictory fashion, of securing a "critical mass" of women, which usually means about 30 percent, not parity.

Since its establishment in 2000, the African Union has adopted some of the most radical texts on gender equality, reaffirmed in the Solemn Declaration on Gender Equality in Africa of 2007, which refers to "gender parity." The European Women's Lobby also started demanding "parity," and linked it to the legitimacy of political institutions in its

2008 campaign, entitled "No Modern European Democracy without Gender Equality." But in order to understand why women are still under-represented, we have to look more deeply into the mechanisms of recruiting candidates.

The "secret garden of politics"

When the voters enter the polling station, the candidates have already been chosen. And, apart from electoral systems based on primaries, voters in general have limited knowledge about how the candidates have been selected. In political science we talk about "the secret garden of politics." In the election, voters can decide the relative strength of the parties; and can, in the case of open or semi-open electoral lists, also cast their vote for specific candidates. But we need to look more closely at the process through which the candidates are selected.

Electoral systems

Electoral systems are not gender-neutral. A global calculation shows that women's parliamentary representation is highest on average (25 percent) under proportional representation electoral systems (PR); lowest in Plurality/Majority (P/M) systems such as those in the USA, UK and India (19 percent); with mixed systems in the middle (22 percent).[4] To understand the differences between the systems, we will need to look at the way the political parties make their nominations.

In most P/M systems there is only one candidate per party in each constituency (single-member districts), and the winner takes all. In PR systems, in contrast, each party presents a list with many candidates in each constituency. This system is more open to newcomers such as women and minorities, because the nominating party does not have to throw out the male incumbent candidate, who always comes first. In P/M systems the nominating local party may fear a negative reaction from (male) voters if the party's only candidate is a woman (majority or minority).

Within the PR system, researchers have looked into whether large electoral districts or large parties in each district – and whether closed or open lists with preferential voting – are best for women's representation. The basic question is whether we assume the political parties or the voters (female voters only?) are likely to be the most supportive of increasing women's representation at a given time.[5] We know that not all women voters vote for female candidates, but what about male voters?

One of the few studies of its kind, a voter survey from Finland which has mandatory preferential voting in a PR system, showed that three-quarters of the male voters practiced "same-gender" voting, (i.e. they voted for a male candidate), while female voters split their votes equally between female and male candidates.[6]

In a mixed system, as for instance in Germany, where half the seats in the Bundestag are elected through PR and the other half through P/M, women get the highest share in the PR section – strong evidence of the varied results from different electoral systems, all other factors being equal. This gender perspective tends to be neglected in the many contemporary constitutional reforms, in which mixed systems are becoming more and more popular, for example under Egypt's new constitution, which has only a fifth of its parliament elected through PR.

Blaming women

From historical studies and from my visits to countries around the world as advisor on the political empowerment of women, I encounter the following type of argument again and again, although in varying forms: it is claimed that women are under-represented because in general terms they are not qualified for political tasks, or that women are not interested in politics or that women do not vote for women. But are these claims valid?

The Kingdom of Bhutan is in a period of transition to democracy. In 2014, I took part in an advisory mission to Bhutan on behalf of the Danish Institute for Parties and Democracy (DIPD), at the invitation of the country's first female government minister, Hon. Ms Dorji Choden, who was also head of the National Commission of Women and Children. The first elections to the National Assembly in 2008 had resulted in the election of only four women (8.5 percent), with a similarly low number at the local elections. There was a serious desire among women's organizations (NGOs) to improve women's representation, perhaps by the use of gender quotas. On a number of occasions during our discussions, we heard that one of the reasons for women's low political representation was that "women do not vote for women." Whenever I hear this argument – and it happens again and again – I feel compelled to ask: "How do you know?" Because of the secrecy of voting, only survey data, which are usually not available, can answer the question of voters' preferences for male or female candidates.

In the case of Bhutan, however, this diagnosis turned out to be wrong. Statistics from the Electoral Commission revealed that in three-quarters of the constituencies there were simply no women candidates. In the remaining constituencies, the success rates for female and male candidates, i.e. the relationship between the percentage nominated and the percentage elected, was almost identical. The example of Bhutan shows how important it is to go one step further back in the electoral process. The main problem was that the political parties had nominated too few women for election, in spite of the many active women in civil society.

Political parties as gatekeepers

The Bhutanese example shows how important it is to ask who selects the candidates – to probe into the secret garden of politics. What are the processes through which candidates are placed high up on party lists for election and/or placed on lists in constituencies where candidates from specific parties have good chances of being elected?

The answer is that in most countries in the world, political parties act as *gatekeepers* to elected posts as well as to many appointed positions in the polity. In some political parties the nomination process is formalized and the proceedings transparent; in others, a small group of party leaders picks the candidates in informal meetings behind closed doors. Feminists have criticized recruitment through "old boy networks" and talked about the "Huey, Dewey and Louie Duck" effect, where those holding the power of recruitment tend primarily to look for people like themselves or people loyal to them. Even in primaries, candidates are usually promoted by powerful networks.

Research has pointed to the importance of women activists within the parties, the degrees of centralization of the party organization, the formalization of recruitment procedures and the party ideology for the representation of women.[7] It is obvious that the level of women's representation is not merely a combined effect of the supply of women candidates, that is, the number of women who are willing to stand for election at a given time, and the demand for women candidates on the part of the political parties. The political parties themselves often explain the low representation of women by pointing to their difficulties in recruiting women, and surveys have shown that men outnumber women as party members and that a higher number of men than women are willing to run for office. However, this explanation neglects the bias in the recruitment system and the dynamic relation between supply and demand: most politicians began their careers when someone in a position of power within a party encouraged them to run. The main problem in politics is the lack of demand, including a lack of long-term strategies on the part of the political parties for greater inclusiveness of under-represented groups, including women, minorities and immigrants.

Ivory Coast, summer 2016. It was during a rather technical conference on how to design a gender quota system for the Ivory Coast, arranged by the Women's Caucus in parliament and its supporters among male MPs, together with the Inter-Parliamentary Union (IPU), that a discussion suddenly broke out about women lacking qualifications for political jobs. This unexpected argument, blaming women for their low representation, came to a halt when the host of the conference, the vice president of the National Assembly, Mme. Fadika Sarra Sako, took the floor and told colleagues her personal story about how it took her years of approaching one male political leader after another before she was accepted as a candidate for the party. She made it clear that it is not just your qualifications that make you a candidate; what you need – in the Ivory Coast's system, as in most other party systems – is

47

the endorsement of powerful men (and women) in the party.

Ideology matters

The differences between political parties within a given country may be just as great as or even greater than differences between neighboring countries. The literature has shown unambiguously that left-wing and Green parties today are more inclusive in relation to women than are right-wing parties. Table 2.4 provides some examples.

Table 2.4. Variations between parties: percentage of women in the party groups in parliament[8]

Australia 28%	UK 29%	Germany 37%	Sweden 43%
Right Coalition 17%	Cons. 21%	CDU/CSU 25%	Moderates 52%
Labor 41%	Labour 43%	Social Dem. 42%	Social Dem. 47%
Others 7%	SNP 36%	Linke (Left) 56%	Left 57%
	Others 50%	Greens 56%	Greens 48%
			3 center parties 35%
			Sweden Democrats 22%

The largest difference in women's representation between left and right parties is found
in the Australian case. Table 2.4 also reveals
why, in contrast, since the 1990s Sweden has
achieved parity for women in parliament (40–60),
because even the Swedish Conservative Party (the
Moderates) has achieved parity within its parliamentary group, while conservative parties in the
other countries in Table 2.4 lag behind the left-
leaning parties (though both the British and the
German conservatives show movement on the
issue).[9]

The new anti-immigration populist parties,
represented in the table by the Sweden Democrats,
deliberately abstain from following the newly established norms of high representation of women,
at least in their first elections. In contrast, from
their initial entrance into parliaments, all over the
world Green parties have set new standards, as
50–50 power-sharing between women and men is
an ideological priority for them, and they often
have two party leaders, one of each gender.[10]
Left-wing Socialist parties also score highly today
on women's representation, while the results for the
large Social Democratic parties are generally good
in this respect – although with variations between
countries.

Incremental versus fast-track development

All in all, many factors have contributed to recent increases in women's political representation. Extensive research has revealed multiple factors – structural as well as actor-oriented – but the conclusion is that there is no single explanation for the variations in the level of women's political representation.[11] And recent developments in the Global South have negated correlations that had previously been found between socio-economic development and the level of women's representation: it is no longer the case that the richer countries have the highest representation of women. This is a remarkable finding.

While the old democracies are now celebrating 100 years of women's suffrage, other countries are wondering if it really has to take 100 years to reach a level of 30–40 percent for women's representation in parliament or local councils. At the end of the 1990s only five countries – Sweden, Denmark, Norway, Finland and the Netherlands – had passed the 30 percent threshold, but today over fifty countries, twenty-three of which are from the Global South (as of the start of 2017), have done so. Worldwide, we know that the leading country is now Rwanda (64 percent), followed by Bolivia (53 percent), and both these countries are examples of the fast-track model.

The traditional *incremental track model*, with its long yet resolute struggle to increase women's representation in old-style parties and in old democracies, is challenged by the new *fast-track model* found in the Global South, not least in *post-conflict* countries in transition to democracy. The conclusion that can be drawn is that the Nordic countries and the Netherlands no longer represent *the* model – at least not the only model – when it comes to strengthening women's political representation.[12] The IPU might in the future just as well place the six countries of the East African Community (EAC) – Burundi, Kenya, Rwanda, South Sudan, Tanzania and Uganda – side by side with the Nordic countries at the top of their usual regional list (see www.ipu.org).

Table 2.5. Two leading regions for women's political representation: percentage of women in parliament (P) and government (G)

	P: 1997	P: 2016	G: 2016
Nordic countries	36	41	43
East African countries	13	32	27

It would be wrong to see the East African countries merely as latecomers compared to the five Nordic countries. While the latter have experienced maximum increases of 8 percent at any election, even during the take-off phase in the 1970s and 1980s, several East African countries have witnessed remarkable leaps in women's representation of 10–20 percent in just one election, not least as a consequence of the adoption of electoral gender quotas by law.

Level of democracy

One would expect women's political representation to be highest in democratic political systems, as was the case previously. Democratic systems are supposed to be more open to pressure from women's organizations and from the voters. We will test this hypothesis against two well-known indexes of democracy. Figure 2.2 confirms that women's representation is highest in democratic states; however, the differences in relation to level of democracy in place are only minor today. According to *Freedom House*, 25, 20 and 22 percent, while *The Economist* index shows a little higher differentiation: 31, 23, 20 and 22 percent

Figure 2.2. Level of democracy and women's parliamentary representation, in percentages

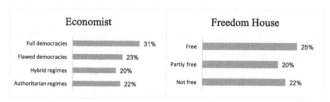

Source: Freedom House, 2016 (for 2015, 195 countries) and the *Economist* Intelligence Unit's Democracy Index 2015 (165 countries). Own calculations, based on IPU figures for women's representation.

from the highest to the lowest level of democracy. It is remarkable – and a new world trend – that authoritarian/not-free regimes have begun to include more women in their usually less powerful legislatures.

The difference between the two indexes – *The Economist*'s 31 percent women among "full democracies" and Freedom House's 25 percent among the "Free" countries – can be explained by variations in the indicators used in the construction of the two indexes.[13] By and large, Figure 2.2 confirms the result of other contemporary studies that women's representation is pretty much the same in democratic and non-democratic regimes – an amazing result.

However, this type of analysis only reflects one point in time. In a longitudinal analysis from 2010, Pamela Paxton, Melanie Hughes and Matthew Painter also found that democracy does not influence the *level* of women's political representation at the start of political liberalization, but it does influence its *growth* over time, as democracy creates conditions for the mobilization of women around the issue of under-representation.[14] In another study, on the sub-Saharan countries, Melanie Hughes and Aili Mari Tripp confirm this result. Their analysis shows that the impressive increase in women's representation in Africa over the past two decades is to be found almost entirely in *post-conflict countries*, while countries with ongoing conflicts and non-conflict countries score lower. They argue that the transformation in the composition of the elites through new constitutions and new political institutions has paved the way for new leaders, including women.[15]

The new democracy in South Africa is one of the most well-known examples: women's representation increased there from 2.7 percent prior to 1994 to 27.7 percent after the first democratic election, mostly thanks to the policy of gender inclusiveness and the many active female leaders of the dominant party, the African National Congress (ANC).

Not all conflicts, however, lead to the dislocation of old elites, and not all elite dislocations affect male dominance, as we saw in the first free elections in Central and Eastern Europe in the 1990s after the collapse of the Soviet Union, where women's parliamentary representation actually dropped.[16]

The first elections following the Arab Uprisings also yielded a disappointing result for women, though with large variations: the lowest in Egypt (2 percent in the 2011–12 election), the highest in Tunisia (27 percent in the 2011 election). In general, male dominance among the elites of the transitional movements, supported by the old patriarchal structures in society, has been of decisive importance. Even if women participated actively in revolutions and uprisings, there were strong forces, including among some of the young activists, wanting to push women back to the domestic sphere. Recent events bear witness to this. During the popular occupation of the parliament building in Moscow in 1993, male activists suddenly started asking the participating women to return home at midnight! Astonishingly, the same thing happened in Tahrir Square twenty years later, but even in this case the women activists refused.

Conclusion

Is the world on the right track towards gender parity? According to the *time-lag theory*, obtaining gender equality is primarily a matter of time, and the successive reaching of thresholds of levels of political representation – first 10 percent, then 25 percent and, at times, over 40 percent – seems to have confirmed this theory. Such optimism has been quite widespread in the public debate, perhaps especially amongst the old democracies.

The modernization theory of Ronald Inglehart and Pippa Norris in *Rising Tide. Gender Equality and Cultural Change Around the World* (2003) lends support to the time-lag theory. Changes in women's and men's lives are related to the development of more egalitarian attitudes in the post-industrial, more secularized societies, as measured in the World Values Survey. Even though Inglehart and Norris have stressed that this is not a matter of simple unidirectional causality, the theory does encompass *predictability* in the broad direction of value change and hence of increases in, among other things, women's political representation.

In contrast, the theory of *continuous reproduction of patriarchal structures* implies that stagnation and even backlash are likely to occur in gender equality and thus also in women's political representation. This theory is supported by the fact that the level of women's representation in many countries tends to fluctuate, and that a certain stagnation has occurred recently. The IPU's 2015 overview states: "Numbers plateau in a year of political turbulence." The future therefore seems unpredictable.

When Joni Lovenduski stated that political representation is a fundamental feminist concern, "although its importance has not always been acknowledged," she might be referring to the argument that women are now just entering institutions of diminishing power: "Women in, then power out." However, this *theory of shrinking institutions* is also heard in an inverse form: "Power out, then women in."[17]

This theory is common in the public debate, but is nevertheless highly contentious, and too vague to be tested empirically. First, the power of elected assemblies varies over time and location for many different reasons. Further, the direction of causality of this theory is unclear, as the two alternative versions of the theory reveal. Indeed, the basic premise can be challenged: one test could be whether men have become less interested in competing for elected posts, something that has not been confirmed. Even when the theory of shrinking institutions is rejected, there are nevertheless many current challenges to the decision-making power of national and local legislatures, which have lost power to regional and global governance structures and because of the last decades' neo-liberalist trends of outsourcing and privatization (to be discussed further in Chapters 4 and 5).

Ever since the achievement of women's suffrage, women politicians have had to adjust to political institutions. With the adoption of gender quotas (to be discussed in the next chapter), crucial structural changes are for the first time being made to and by the political institutions in order to facilitate the inclusion of women. This is new – and highly controversial.

3

The Impact of Gender Quotas

Why are gender quotas in politics so controversial? Do quotas, as the heated debates indicate, challenge some of the fundamental structures which uphold male dominance in politics? According to opponents, gender quotas violate vital democratic principles. The proponents, on their side, see women's continual under-representation as an indication of how democracy – in fact all political systems – have continued to fail women and, consequently, why new and more effective measures are needed.

No one had predicted the rapid spread of gender quotas in electoral systems to over half the countries in the world.[1] Today, more than eighty countries as diverse as Bolivia, South Korea, India, France and Uganda have by law adopted gender quotas for their elected assemblies in order to improve women's political representation. In an additional forty or so countries some political parties, most often Green and Left parties, have adopted such quotas for their own electoral lists, with Sweden and South Africa being among the most successful examples.[2] This implies that in over half the countries of the world some type of quota provisions is at work.

The first part of this chapter disentangles the different gender quota systems and analyzes the various discourses about them. We look at all of the contrasting predictions in relation to actual experience. In the second part of the chapter, the recent global spread of electoral quotas for women is traced and analyzed, and at the end of the chapter we examine the puzzle: why have so many parliaments in the world, all with a majority of male MPs, adopted gender quotas, in a move seemingly contrary to their own interests?

It is argued in this chapter that the extent to which electoral gender quotas are a violation of the principle of merit and the principle of election through competition – or, on the contrary, can contribute to processes of democratization – depends on how women's continued under-representation is explained, as well as how the quota rules are constructed.

The Impact of Gender Quotas

The new top of the world

Table 3.1 shows the top fifteen countries in terms of women's representation in parliament (single chamber or lower chamber). Ten of the fifteen countries presently topping the list are Global South countries, while five are from the Global North. Table 3.1 also shows that the majority of the countries at the top end use proportional representation (PR) electoral systems, which, as we saw in the last chapter, are in general more open to the inclusion of women; and that all of the Global South countries at the top of the list have adopted some kind of electoral gender quotas in law in accordance with the *fast-track model*.

Even most of the European countries topping the list today make use of gender quotas. However, most are voluntary quotas by the political parties (see definitions below). Finland is the only one among the top-ranking countries that has attained such a high level of women's representation without any quota provisions.[3]

Defining quotas

Everyone has an opinion about gender quotas. However, few, even among lawmakers and quota

The Impact of Gender Quotas

Table 3.1. Women in parliament: top-ranking countries

Country	Women in parliament	Election year	Quotas	Electoral system
1. Rwanda	64.0	2013	Legislated quotas	PR
2. Bolivia	53.1	2014	Legislated quotas	Mixed
3. Cuba	48.9	2013	NA	One party
4. Iceland	47.6	2016	Party quotas	PR
5. Nicaragua	45.7	2016	Legislated quotas	PR
6. Sweden	43.5	2014	Party quotas	PR
7. Senegal	42.7	2012	Legislated quotas	Mixed
8. Mexico	42.4	2015	Legislated quotas	Mixed
9. Ecuador	41.6	2013	Party quotas	PR
10. Finland	41.5	2015	No quotas	PR
11. Namibia	41.3	2014	Party quotas	PR
12. South Africa	40.8	2014	Party quotas	PR
13. Mozambique	39.6	2014	Party quotas	PR
14. Norway	39.6	2013	Party quotas	PR
15. Belgium	39.3	2014	Legislated quotas	PR

Source: www.ipu.org, January 2017. Election-day figures are here combined with data on electoral systems and quota regimes. "Legislated quotas" means quotas mandated in the constitution, electoral law, party law etc. Party quotas are regulations adopted by individual parties for their own electoral lists. In percentages.

advocates, know exactly how they work. Electoral gender quotas can be defined as an affirmative-action measure, which stipulates that there should be a certain number or proportion of women among those nominated or elected. Gender quotas are thus about numbers or percentages. It is a fast-track policy designed to remedy an undesirable inequality. Gender quotas can be for women or – which is more common – gender-neutral, setting a minimum and a maximum for each sex, for example 30–70 percent or 40–60 percent. Below are the three main types of electoral gender quotas, with some examples:

1. Party candidate quotas – adopted by individual parties

Sweden: there is no legal requirement for quotas, but the Greens, the Left Socialists and the Social Democratic Party apply the "zipper system," that is, they nominate 50 percent men and 50 percent women on their lists for election, alternating between men and women throughout the list. The other political parties work mostly with softer recommendations. The contested All-Women Short List of the British Labour Party, which gave priority to women in filling certain vacant seats, is another sort of voluntary party quota. A requirement of

30–40 percent of each gender on the lists is most widespread.

2. Legislated candidate quotas
Argentina: the law requires that all parties have at least 30 percent women among the candidates on their lists, and requires at least one woman candidate for every two men throughout the list.

3. Reserved seat, mandated in constitution or law
Reserved seat quotas can take many forms, but they all regulate the number of women (and perhaps even other groups) among those elected.
Morocco: sixty of 395 seats are reserved for women and thirty seats for young people (of both sexes under forty) and they are elected by all voters on the basis of special national lists. The voters thus have two votes: one for the national list and one for the district seats. The first four elections with quotas resulted in 11, 11, 17 and 21 percent of women elected. There was regret that very few women were nominated and elected to the non-reserved general district seats (PR).[4]
India, local government: according to a constitutional amendment of 1993, 33 percent of the seats are reserved for women, elected in women-candidate-only elections by all of the voters of both sexes. The reserved seats rotate among the villages

from election to election. In addition, among the seats reserved for scheduled castes, at least 33 percent are for women, and 33 percent of the chairpersons have to be women. The result is that around 1 million women per electoral cycle serve in the local councils, the Panchayats (P/M).

A few countries, among them Rwanda, combine reserved seats with candidate quotas. In Rwanda two women per province are elected by a special electorate consisting of local councilors and women's organizations. The rest of the parliament is elected in district elections based on a closed-list PR system, where at least 30 percent of the candidates must be women.

Most liberal and right-wing parties find quotas "illiberal," and prefer to operate on the basis of less binding quota recommendations, the so-called *soft quotas*, if any at all.

Candidate quotas are most common in proportional representation (PR) electoral systems. For how can a party nominate 30 to 40 percent women when each party only has one candidate per district? France (P/M) and Bolivia (Mixed) are among the exceptions. They have tried to solve the problem through provisions that each party nominate 50 percent female and 50 percent male candidates in the single-member districts for the entire country taken together – so-called horizontal quotas. Because quotas are more easily applied to a PR system, the discrepancy between PR and P/M electoral systems in terms of women's representation will probably become even greater in the future following the adoption of quotas by even more countries. *Rank order rules*, also called placement mandates, are crucial for the outcome of candidate quotas. Even a 30 to 40 percent candidate requirement can result in no women being elected, if all of the female candidates are placed at the bottom of the party lists in a PR election or in weak constituencies for their party in single-member districts.

Legal sanctions for non-compliance have also proved to be crucial, being most effective if the electoral authorities in such cases have the mandate to reject lists. Financial penalties are usually not effective sanctions, since the largest (and richest) parties may not care, as we saw in France where the 50–50 parity legislation in the first election in 2002 only resulted in 12 percent of women in the National Assembly, although it rose to 18 and 26 percent in 2007 and 2012 respectively.

Tunisia 2011. The revolution that ousted President Ben Ali has so far resulted in the most sustainable new political system emerging from the Arab Uprisings, even from a gender perspective, though many inequalities still remain. Our IPU-advisory delegation of three, which included the French feminist politician Françoise Gaspard, the Gender Programme Officer Zeina Hilal from IPU's headquarters in Geneva, and myself, was invited by the Council for the Realization of the Goals of the Revolution, Political Reform and Democratic Transition, which was to formulate a draft of a new electoral law for the election of the first Constitutional Assembly. It was a surprise to learn that the Council had already decided on a PR electoral system based on the radical "zipper system." The only thing left for us to advocate was the removal of an Article which stated that if the political parties could not find enough women, they did not have to comply with the rules. This was wisely dropped, since the whole idea of a gender quota system is to force the political parties to look more seriously for potential women candidates.

Why did this radical quota system only result in 27 percent women being elected? It was the best result in the region at that time, but feminists were disappointed, as Tunisia had already had 28 percent of women in parliament under Ben Ali. The reason for this result of 27 percent was that, after the ban on Ben Ali's party, Constitutional Democratic Rally (CDR), more than eighty new parties stood for election. All of them, with the exception of the winning moderate Islamist Ennahda Party, won either no seats or just one seat per electoral district, and almost all of the lists (93 percent) were topped by a man with a woman as the list's number two. This improved somewhat in the following election in 2014, which resulted in 31 percent women being elected, yet it was still far from the goal of parity.

Quota discourses

Following Carol Bacchi's analysis in her "What's the problem" approach, we can identify different diagnoses of the problem of "why women are under-represented" that underlie the different positions on electoral gender quotas. The traditionalists will deny that there is any problem of "under-representation" – otherwise, their resistance to quotas could rest on the conviction that this is the result of women's own choices. Disagreements are to be found, though, even among feminists, since some fear that women elected because of gender quotas could be stigmatized as "quota women."

The Impact of Gender Quotas

Carol Bacchi criticizes the use of the concepts "positive discrimination," "special treatment" or "specific advantage" – concepts used by both opponents and advocates. Affirmative action can be seen as "an attempt to redress entrenched privilege." From this perspective, quotas are not discriminatory, in a positive or a negative way, or preferential treatment. They are a way of doing justice, according to Bacchi.[5]

This alternative perspective, which I also share, represents a shift away from a discourse about women themselves, which could result in a fear of "essentializing" women, to a debate about exclusions and inequalities in the institutions. From this it follows that if everything was fair in society and no barriers existed for one or the other gender, then it would be reasonable to consider quotas unfair.

International organizations, such as the United Nations, the European Union and the African Union, increasingly support affirmative-action policies, even if the controversial term "quotas" is usually avoided. The UN Convention on the Elimination of All Forms of Discrimination against Women (CEDAW) from 1979 uses the term "temporary special measures" (TSM). The UN Platform for Action, in Beijing in 1995, does not mention the word "quotas." However, as we saw earlier, the

Declaration does speak of "discriminatory attitudes and practices" and "unequal power relations" in accordance with the fast-track discourse.

Not all legislators would follow Bacchi's theoretical reasoning; however, the legitimacy of these Declarations derives from the fact that they have been signed by most of the governments of the world – although with reservations on the part of some. During my missions around the world, I have witnessed very many cases, such as in the Polish parliament, where leading national politicians are so to speak *squeezed* – in the face of full media coverage – between domestic women's NGOs that advocate gender quotas, and transnational feminist organizations and gender experts, who all refer to UN Declarations.

Predictions and results

It is remarkable that the same arguments for and against quotas are repeated in all corners of the world. A closer look also reveals that, in spite of all of the experiences and all of the research to hand, these arguments often take the form of *predictions* about what is supposed to happen after the introduction of gender quotas.

Table 3.2 sets out the most well-known arguments for and against electoral gender quotas and how

The Impact of Gender Quotas

Table 3.2. Seven arguments for and against quotas[6]

Opponents' predictions	Proponents' predictions
Descriptive representation	
1. Quotas are unnecessary, as women's representation will gradually increase in a natural way. 2. It will not be possible to find a sufficient number of (qualified) women. Women will not want to be selected because of their sex. 3. Quotas are a violation of the free choice of the voters, are demeaning to women and will undermine the principle of merit.	1. Quotas are necessary in order to achieve a rapid increase in women's political representation. 2. There will be a sufficient number of qualified women candidates, if political parties begin to look more seriously for women. 3. Quotas will contribute to enlarging the pool of potential candidates and thus make much better use of diverse qualifications in society.
Substantive representation	
4. Women elected via quotas will only be seen as "quota women," and their political effectiveness will, consequently, be limited. 5. Quota women will be regarded as "token" or "proxy" women, too dependent on their party leaders or husbands.	4. A critical mass of women will bring a different style and approach to politics. 5. A critical mass of women will be able to introduce new policy concerns onto the political agenda.
Symbolic representation	
6. After gender quotas, other groups will start demanding quotas, such as ethnic minorities, left-handed people, even redheads! 7. Quotas only treat the symptoms of women's under-representation and therefore will only be a symbolic gesture.	6. Gender is one of the most important axes of power in society. Gender quotas are therefore not only necessary but essential. 7. Quotas will contribute to the process of democratization by opening up the "secret garden of politics."

The Impact of Gender Quotas

they are related to the three dimensions of women's political representation: descriptive representation (the numbers), substantive representation (the policies) and symbolic representation (the meaning attached to representation).

Some of these predictions can be tested against actual experience, for instance No. 2 and No. 3 in the table on page 71, while others can only be properly judged in a longitudinal perspective, for instance No. 7. Some need to be transformed into more precise hypotheses. We have seen how researchers can differ in their evaluations of quotas, sometimes because they write about different countries or, as in the strikingly different evaluations of the actual influence of the many female politicians in Rwanda, because of unclear or disparate criteria for evaluation.[7] We can only touch on some of these predictions here, but encourage the readers to try them out against what is known about the impact of gender quotas in their own country.

The natural order

The first argument (No. 1 in Table 3.2) considers the fast-track model versus the incremental track model. Both camps can find support in actual developments, as we saw earlier. No. 2, however, can be tested empirically. Thus far, reports of a lack of female candidates come primarily from the political parties involved in local elections, and less often in parliamentary elections. Quotas violate the "free choice" of the voters, opponents argue (No. 3). To this, the proponents respond that there is nothing "natural" about the existing order and that this is a typical, long-standing argument on the part of the elite in order to retain their own positions of power. The argument about the free choice of the voters also seems less convincing, since political parties in their role as gatekeepers for elected positions often leave voters little choice, in particular in systems with closed electoral lists where voters can only cast their votes for parties, not for individual candidates. In many countries the candidates' names are not even printed on the ballot paper.

Merits

Predictions No. 2 and No. 3 are related to the widespread debate about merits and "unqualified quota women." It seems that this argument is put forward in particular in relation to women, since it is seldom used for male candidates or, for example, candidates nominated because the party needs someone on the list from the northern or southern part of a constituency. Women's rights advocates all over the world respond to this with a question: "How qualified are the men who presently occupy the seats?"

Susan Franceschet and Jennifer M. Piscopo[8] have analyzed the truth behind the accusation that women parliamentarians in Argentina are less qualified following the adoption of the quota law. This research confirmed similar findings in other countries that male and female parliamentarians do have distinct profiles but, in general, have the same level of education. In some countries in Asia, women parliamentarians are in fact more highly educated than the men. The double bind they encounter is also illustrated in the case of Argentina, where the women MPs, if more well educated, are criticized for belonging to the political elite.

British political scientist Rainbow Murray has suggested that, instead of talking about quotas for women, we should start discussing *quotas for men* – because it is the over-representation of men that is the problem. Murray argues that this will shift the usual intense scrutiny of women's qualifications to an examination of men's credentials. All citizens would benefit from "ceiling quotas" for men, she argues, since this will broaden the talent pool and lead to true meritocracy, as *both* genders will be scrutinized.[9]

"Tokens"

In the Argentinian case, women MPs were also accused of being "tokens," that is, for not having their own agenda. In India, local female councilors elected on the basis of reserved seats are accused of being "proxy" women – simply stand-ins for their husbands (No. 5 in Table 3.2). There are reports of cases where a husband even at first took the seat that his wife had won in the women-only election. It felt like a cultural revolution when, at a meeting in New Delhi for over 1,000 female councilors, organized by the Institute for Social Science, I heard a woman stand up and tell us all quite openly that she had indeed had problems with her husband and her in-laws when she took her seat. "But then I say to my husband: all right, you are still the head of the household, but I am the head of the Council!"

The democratic legitimacy of being elected under a quota system

Opponents of quotas often question the democratic legitimacy of being elected under a quota system. This is a genuine concern for women parliamentarians, also shared by many feminists. Yet, ever since enfranchisement, female politicians have been accused of being nominated or elected "just because you are a woman," while male politicians are never asked the same question, despite the obvious advantages for men in many phases of the selection process.

The legitimacy of quota systems should depend on the extent to which the MPs or local councilors have won their seats *in open competition*. That is, of course, usually the case with candidate quotas, which do not guarantee election. Reserved seat quotas (RS) are seen as more problematic. Today, however, most reserved seats systems – in contrast to previous traditions of appointment – are based on elections. In principle, the number of seats in RS systems is fixed for women as a group, while the individual female politicians are scrutinized by the voters in open competition with other women candidates. And yet it may be considered to be a democratic problem when men are excluded *de jure* from competing for certain seats. The feminist response is that most elections have *de facto* been based on competition between men only.

Gender, ethnicity and class

According to a well-worn argument by quota opponents (see No. 6 in Table 3.2), gender quotas will lead to endless demands for quotas on the part of various other groups. It should be noted, however, that many formal and even informal quotas are already at work when parties nominate their candidates. Reservations for national minorities, such as the two seats reserved for the German minority in the Polish parliament, have been in place for a long time and are usually attached to particular geographic areas. Class quotas have, since the days of the old estates, become rare, though Egypt, ever since Nasser's regime, has a radical 50 percent reservation for "workers and farmers," enshrined also in the newest electoral law and much less discussed than quotas for women. Quotas for ethnic minorities are a more recent occurrence, often adopted as a post-conflict instrument. Immigrants are grossly under-represented everywhere, but it is, as British political scientist Anne Phillips argues, extremely difficult to formally define the relevant constituencies.[10] An interesting conclusion from a series of interviews made within the frame of the large FEMCIT project on "Gendered Citizenship in Multicultural Europe," with *women's minority organizations* in Warsaw, Skopje, Stockholm, London and Madrid, about their preferred representation and the issue of quotas, was that they all – with the exception of Muslim women's organizations in London – wanted a general gender quota, but not ethnic quotas.[11]

In the second part of this chapter, we will follow the development of gender quotas. What have been the driving forces behind the global spread of electoral gender quotas?[12]

First, second and third quota waves

It is possible to identify three waves of gender quota regulations. The early *first wave* saw the use of different types of gender quotas in many of the Communist countries, as well as in Pakistan after 1956 and Bangladesh after 1972 (with some interruptions in both of these countries) and Egypt in 1979–84 – all, however, quite unpopular.

In the Nordic countries, voluntary party quotas were introduced during the strong feminist mobilization in the 1970s and 1980s, beginning with left-wing and Green parties, who adopted quotas for their own internal executive bodies and their electoral lists.[13]

The *second wave* began with the introduction of the above-mentioned quota law in Argentina in 1991, and this then became the model for the subsequent spread of gender quotas all over Latin America.[14] For the following two decades, we see the continuous adoption of quotas by more countries, reaching a high point after the Beijing World Conference on Women in 1995 and most recently following the criticism concerning the lack of fulfillment of the Millennium Development Goals (MDGs).

Most countries with gender quotas for their single chamber or lower chamber have also adopted gender quotas for sub-national assemblies, including regional and local councils and, to a somewhat lesser extent, for the upper chambers. The most recent development can be followed on the global website: www.quotaproject.org.[15]

In 43 percent of all countries, including the USA and Russia, however, there are no quota provisions, neither legislated nor party quotas. Reserved seat quota provisions are mainly found in Asia, the Middle East and North Africa, as well as in some countries in East Africa, which often have majoritarian electoral systems in place. Legislated candidate quotas are the preferred gender quota type in Latin America, parts of Europe and Africa. Party quotas are found most predominantly in Southern Africa and Europe. Among the twenty-eight Member States of the European Union, the following six (in order of adoption) changed from party quotas of individual parties to quota laws binding for all political parties: France, Belgium, Portugal, Slovenia, Spain, Croatia and Poland.

Driving forces

What have been the driving forces behind quota adoption? An investigation based on the Gender Quota Database (GQD), Stockholm University, 2014, which includes 196 countries (multifactor analyses, logistic regression), indicates that the following structural conditions lead to quota adoption (only quotas by law are included).

First, *regional adoption of gender quotas by law*, especially among neighboring states, has been of importance. Second, *international forces* also turned out to be important for quota adoption, indicating the importance of interaction with the international community and with donor-country agencies as well as the growing support for stronger affirmative action provisions on the part of *transnational feminism*. Third, *domestic women's movements and intervention by women in political parties* has proved to be significant, suggesting that quotas are not simply imposed on countries as a result of external pressures by Western donors or regional organizations. In general, these results are in line with previous research on factors behind quota adoption as well as with experiences from our consultancies around the world.

This analysis confirms that gender quotas are being adopted in *all kinds of societies*. It is remarkable that, according to this analysis, quota adoption has turned out to be unaffected by a number of structural factors, including the level of economic development, the predominant religion, the gender ratio in schools, women in the labor force, and even the level of democratization.

The effectiveness of gender quotas

Do gender quotas have the effect that quota advocates had hoped for – and that some reluctant politicians perhaps feared?

The study shows that the starting point in a majority of all countries (51 percent) with quota laws was women's representation of below 10 percent in the last elections prior to quota adoption – no doubt this low level served as an incentive to adopt quotas. A quarter (26 percent) had 10–19 percent female MPs before quotas. This study can show the effects of the quota laws, as we can see in Table 3.3, measured by the first electoral result following the quota legislation.

These first results were often disappointing for the quota advocates, since almost half the countries (44 percent) experienced no increase or only a very modest one (<5 percent) in the first election after the quota provision took effect. Ten countries experienced a decrease, no doubt

Table 3.3. Immediate effect of quota laws on women's parliamentary representation and on quota law revision

Change in the proportion of women after the first quota law (in percentage points)	Total number of countries (N)		Hereof countries that have amended the original quota law	
	N	%	N	%
Decrease	10	12.8	4	11.4
No change	1	1.3	1	2.9
Increase < 5%	23	29.5	12	34.3
Increase 5–9.99%	9	11.5	5	14.2
Increase 10–19.99%	14	18.0	7	20.0
Increase >20%	6	7.7	3	8.6
No previous election	3	3.8	1	2.9
Elections not held yet	10	12.8	–	–
N/A	2	2.5	27	5.7
N=	78	100	35	100

Note: Italy and Venezuela are omitted as the only countries that have abolished their quota laws for national parliament.
Source: The Gender Quotas Database (GQD). Release May 1 2014, Stockholm University.

caused by other factors, but in combination with an unambitious quota law, such as the 5 percent quota for women candidates in Armenia. The independent effects of the first quota laws follow, first and foremost, from how these initial laws were constructed.

However, the other half of the quota countries (56 percent) experienced an increase of between 5 and over 20 percent. In the latter category we find the real fast-track countries, including Rwanda, with its historical leap in 2003 of 23 percent to the top of the world rank order, and Senegal, with a 20 percent leap. In general, the reserved seat electoral systems did a little better than systems with legislated candidate quotas, following the more decisive character of reserved seats.

Table 3.3 links the first results to the likelihood that a country will later amend its quota law. Given the complexity of electoral systems and quota systems, many lawmakers and also many women's rights activists did not initially realize that a 30 percent candidate quota without rank order provisions does not guarantee that 30 percent will be elected. We can also find examples of good intentions, but badly designed laws. Thus we can now witness the *third wave* of quota revisions, most of which strengthen the quota provisions, for instance by raising the quota percentage, by adopting rank order rules or by introducing stronger sanctions for non-compliance or "creative quota designs."[16] Most remarkable, however, are six countries that have strengthened their quota laws, even if the increase after the first law exceeded 20 percent. One of them, Mexico, has strengthened its quota law several times.

Party quotas can also have a considerable effect, in both a short-term and a long-term perspective. Take the example of the large Social Democratic/ Labour parties among the old democracies. The percentage of women in their parliamentary groups increased in the first election after quota adoption as follows (with year of adoption in brackets): Netherlands (1987) from 19 to 31 percent; Germany (1988) from 16 to 27 percent; Sweden (1993) from 41 to 48 percent; and the United Kingdom (1994) from 14 to 24 percent.[17] In all of the countries, the high level attained has either been maintained or raised even further.

Quotas in non-democratic countries

Does it really make sense to work for gender quotas and more women in parliamentary assemblies in non-democratic countries, many feminists outside these countries ask? However, within semi-democratic and non-democratic countries, women's rights advocates today work hard – with some success – by putting pressure on their political leaders to increase women's representation, including through gender quotas. Once the political leader is convinced, it may even prove easier to have gender quotas adopted in less democratic countries with one dominant party, as the examples of Rwanda and Algeria have shown.

Algeria, December 2013. Through its new quota law, Algeria surpassed Tunisia as number one in North Africa and the Middle East, with 32 percent women in the National Assembly, a gigantic leap from only 8 percent in the previous election. I was invited as one of several foreign speakers to a high-level conference on women in elected assemblies, organized by the parliament and the Ministry of Foreign Affairs and supported by the UN. The quota law was passed in 2012 against the background of the Uprisings in other Arab countries, but had been prepared by a Commission led by influential women in the state apparatus. When the President decided in the end to support quotas, resistance in the dominant FLN Party (National Liberation Front) was finally eliminated. And here they were, all of the 146 female MPs – typically, the local doctor, veterinarian or teacher, and most of them recruited to national politics for the first time. At the conference, some Algerian feminists based in the capital protested loudly: "Women did not fight for the quota, it was imposed from above." "Too many of the female MPs come from the countryside, only a few from the big cities." It was obvious that the militant feminists saw the elected women as tokens for the dominant party. The law reserved a third of the seats for women on all electoral lists but differentiated between 20 and 50 percent, according to the size of the constituencies, with the lowest reservations in the countryside. This formulation led to a dispute after the election: was this regulation of the candidates or of those elected, i.e. candidate quotas or reserved seats? In the end, the latter interpretation was chosen, which meant that many women ranked lower on the lists were declared elected – a controversial measure.

In her book *Political Institutions under Dictatorships* (2008), American political scientist Jennifer Gandhi asserted that founding legislative and partisan institutions on some type of formal election is important for regime survival as a means of neutralizing threats from the opposition. However, we need more research on the type of bargaining power women's rights advocates have at their disposal in non-democratic regimes. Women's rights activists in non-democratic countries, as in the case of Algeria, maintain that they find some openings for the representation of women today: first, because gender issues are not considered "real" politics and are therefore seen as less dangerous; second, because political leaders accept quotas in order to appear modern and more "democratic" in today's world; and third, because the political leaders of dominant parties reckon that loyal women will be elected, as in Algeria.

Such considerations go some way to answer the puzzle presented at the start of this chapter: why do male-dominated parliaments pass quota laws at all? We are now moving into the difficult field of interpreting motives, which, especially in the case of quotas, are often very mixed. To the three motives just mentioned, we can add the following, which are also relevant for democratic countries: fourth, ideological support for the cause of women's empowerment; fifth, admitting to the strong mobilization of women/feminists in civil society and inside the political parties, and to quota advocates within the political elite; and finally, in democratic countries, vote-maximizing motives in the electoral competition between parties (though that also requires a certain level of feminist awareness among voters).

The Impact of Gender Quotas

A short guide to gender quota advocates

1. The time to ask nicely for "more women in politics" is over. Precise targets and strategies are the agenda of today.

2. The choice of quota system for your country should be selected to suit the political and electoral system in place. Look at the experience of other countries with similar systems. Don't start from scratch. Consult the global website www.quotaprojects.org.

3. The devil is in the details. Go for precise and ambitious quota provisions, including rank order rules to guarantee that the female candidates are not just placed in unwinnable positions. Apply sanctions for non-compliance.

4. Remember that the political parties are the real gatekeepers to elected positions. Demand 50 percent women in the candidate selection committee, even in systems with primaries. If there is no such committee, demand that one be established.

5. Have realistic expectations. Gender quotas are no miracle cure for all barriers that women face in politics, such as lack of campaign financing, harassment and intimidation during campaigning, plus the problems of combining political life with work and family obligations.

Conclusion

Gender quotas cannot solve all the problems women encounter in politics. However, properly constructed, electoral gender quotas are an effective measure to increase women's numerical representation, since they can help women to surmount the barriers embedded in cultural biases against women candidates and the traditional methods of recruitment through old-boy networks. But in general, sustainable and effective quotas depend on the mobilization of women's organizations and networks, prior, under and after the adoption.

Can quotas contribute to democratization in countries in transition? And can they improve the functioning of long-standing democracies in crisis as a result of increasing distrust on the part of the citizens toward the political institutions, including the political parties? The answer to the first part of the question relates to the "who" of democracy since, by effectively changing women's historical under-representation, electoral gender quotas can contribute to democratization in terms of who is included in political decision-making in all types of societies. Second, gender quotas in elections also play a part in reforming the "how" of democracy, that is, the structure of the political system, by opening up the "secret garden of politics." At best, nomination processes can be made more formalized and transparent.

When Anne Phillips states, in *The Politics of Presence* (1995), that her intention is not to exchange the traditional "politics of ideas" for a "politics of presence" but to combine them, she could have taken her argument one step further: introducing gender quotas in a party system with a variety of programs, forcing all parties to increase their representation of women and other under-represented groups, would create such a combination of ideas and presence.

In conclusion, if the diagnosis of women's under-representation finds *de facto* special treatment that favors males – or white men, as opposed to both "women" and "minorities" – then the use of quotas is not a violation of the principle of liberal democracy or discrimination against men, but compensation to women or others for the discrimination they meet in politics.

Some feminist advocates see electoral gender quotas as a means to increase women's representation as a goal in itself because of its high symbolic value. However, as we saw earlier, most campaigns for increasing women's political representation expect women in politics to make a difference. Gender quota advocates add the expectation that women's power will increase when they become a "critical mass" in politics. The next chapter will look at the potential fulfillment of those expectations.

4

Gendering Public Policy

Olof Palme, the Swedish Social Democratic prime minister (1969–76 and 1982–6), maintained that it was only fair that the working class, through the Social Democratic Party, had control of the government in Sweden for much of the period from the 1930s onwards, as this balanced the control the bourgeoisie had over the economy and most of the press! If this rationale was to be applied to gender relations, the argument would go like this: as long as the market, academia and even the streets at night are controlled by men, it seems only fair that women should have control over the political institutions. In reality, no campaign for "more women in politics" has demanded more than *parity*, that is, power-sharing.

Public policy-making is never gender-neutral, as long as women and men, including specific groups of men and women, lead such different lives. This book's broad definition of male dominance in politics (see Table 2.2) leads to a critique of norms and practices in public policy-making, and how public policy fails women and gender equality. Thus women's movements and feminist scholarship call for a *gendering of all public policy*. This chapter will discuss what that implies. Firstly, this chapter will discuss whether women make a difference in politics. To answer this question we need to scrutinize the very concepts of women's interests and gender equality. We will also look critically at the "critical mass theory," which deals with the relation between the descriptive representation of women (the numbers) and the substantive representation (endorsing gender equality policies). Second, we will proceed to look at the growing number of women in leadership positions, their portfolios and commitment to gender equality. Finally, the feminist ambivalence towards gender equality policy, the new so-called "state feminism" is discussed. The chapter will conclude that, in spite of justified criticism of contemporary gender equality policies, women from all walks of life need, in principle, state intervention to counteract patriarchal norms in civil society and the discriminatory effects of the marked forces.

"Blair's Babes"

It was a major breakthrough when 101 Labour women MPs were elected to the British House of Commons in 1997, following the party's landslide election victory. The picture of Tony Blair with all these female MPs on the steps of Church House in Westminster appeared throughout the press and media at the time. Then someone started calling them "Blair's Babes," a highly contested label.

It was indeed a victory for quota regulation in the form of all-women shortlists in the Labour Party, implying that in half of the vacant seats in its parliamentary group, only women could compete for nomination. Expectations were raised because women now made up 18 percent of MPs in the House of Commons. But "Blair's Babes" were subject to sexist attacks and ridicule in the press, and their qualifications were questioned. Most challenging of all was the fact that many feminists expressed their disappointment, not least when the female Labour MPs followed the party whip and voted for budget cuts on lone mother benefits. The media criticized them for concentrating too much on changing their own working conditions in parliament, for instance their claim to be allowed to breastfeed in all rooms of parliament. This constituted a considerable backlash against the incomers, according to Joni Lovenduski: "It is illustrative of how, on the one hand, women politicians are expected to make a difference and are criticized for not transforming centuries of male-designed traditions of politics. But, on the other hand, they are expected to fit in with the culture of the institution and prove themselves according to criteria developed during its long history as a male institution."[1]

What are women's interests?

The concept of "substantive representation" addresses the relationship between the represented and their representatives, in this case women. In her classic book *The Concept of Representation* (1967), Hanna Pitkin talks about the importance of representation as "a substantive" activity – it is a "substantive acting for" others.[2] But Pitkin does not discuss the relationship between descriptive and substantive representation, which has now become a central theme in gender and politics research. Most women's organizations claim that *women's representation* should mean *representing women*, not just creating symbolic representation and career opportunities for the few. It should be a question of commitment as implied in the following quotation from a speech made by Frene Ginwala, when in 1994 she stepped down as leader of the largest national women's organization ever in South Africa, the Women's National Coalition (WNC), to take up her position as Speaker of the first democratic parliament: *"I am woman: my concerns, my problems, my difficulties, my achievements are an integral part of our new society. No one will succeed in marginalizing them or me. I am woman. I am South African. I am me. I go to Parliament but I am woman."*[3]

Shireen Hassim and Anne Marie Goetz, who quote Frene Ginwala, speak about *effectiveness* as the capacity of women politicians to mobilize support in their parties and in civil society for their policy agendas, in particular their capacity to promote gender equality.[4] Women politicians are often squeezed between the demands arising from women's organizations in civil society, their duties as representatives of their constituency and their duty to their party, as in the case of "Blair's Babes." The context is crucial. Many women politicians have told of the negative reactions they receive when raising issues of gender equality. At the same time we know that not all women are feminists and not all feminists are women, which further complicates the question of whom female politicians are representing, both in theory and in practice.

Theoretical dilemmas

At the same time as we see a worldwide demand for equal political representation for women, there is fundamental discussion within feminist theory about the categories "women" and "gender." Judith Butler is one of the post-structuralist feminists who has criticized the feminist movement most strongly for seeking political representation for some assumed "existing identity, understood through the category of women," that initiates feminist interests.[5] It is argued that there is a risk of reinforcing the category of "women," which feminism has tried to get away from, and of "essentializing" women.

In contrast, Anna Jónasdóttir and Kathleen Jones argue that women across the political spectrum have a common interest in being part of the deliberations of political assemblies (in Latin to be *inter esse*), and they criticize post-structuralist feminist theory for confusing epistemological and ontological levels of analysis with empirical science.[6] One could add that if the feminist movement, as described in this book, is not considered primarily as an identity movement, but as a political movement attempting to change male dominance, then there is a need to speak of "women," including diverse groups of women.

In an attempt to solve the theoretical controversies about what constitutes women's interests, Karen Beckwith has introduced a useful distinction between *interests*, *issues* and *preferences*.[7] Women's *interests* are the most fundamental and derive from similar, shared experiences, which differ from those of men. Women's *interests* are constructed in specific instances by political, economic and social arrangements. Intersectional disputes predominantly among women indicate that women's interests are at stake, according to Beckwith. In contrast, *issues* are more specific, immediate and limited, while *preferences* are the strategic alternatives. Beckwith uses the issue of freedom from violence against women as an example of a fundamental *interest*, under which, secondly, the prioritized *issues* may be spousal assault or rape or sexual harassment, whereas, third, there can be an endless range of *preferences*, on which, one may add, various feminisms (in the plural), for instance liberal, socialist, existentialist, radical, post-modern and post-colonial feminisms, will differ.

Iris Marion Young moved the discussion in a fruitful direction in *Inclusion and Democracy*

(2000). She sees representing as *speaking for*, not *speaking as*. From her deliberative perspective, representation is a dynamic process: not representation of some fixed, static ("essentialist") notion of women and women's interests, but an active process that moves between the represented and the representatives.

One strategy for empirical research could be to take as the point of departure the actual claims of various women's organizations and then study the response from the political institutions, including from female and male politicians. Another option could be to study the interventions made by women politicians themselves, looking at what Karen Celis calls "subjectively defined interests."[8] None of these approaches needs an a priori theoretical definition of women's interests.

Ramallah, Palestine 2007. In a private conversation, the female minister from the Fatah party in the Palestinian Authority complained to me, as an expert on gender quotas, about the many Hamas women who had been elected to what was then a united Assembly because of the new gender quotas. However, we soon agreed that, without the quotas, the Hamas group in the Assembly would probably have consisted only of male politicians, and soon the conversation turned into a discussion of possible common interests among the women politicians in spite of their different political affiliations. The minister responded that there were two issues on which it was possible for female Fatah politicians to work together with their Hamas counterparts: policies to counteract violence against women, and girls' education.

Gendering politics

Gendering policy implies looking at all public policy from the perspectives of gender equality. During the recent decades, gender equality policy all over the world has been institutionalized with its own governmental units, commissions and boards, and even ministers for women and children or for gender equality. Gender equality laws, including equal pay provisions, anti-discrimination regulations and actions against violence against women have been adopted in a large number of countries. In contemporary global discourses, the term "women's interests" has been replaced by new concepts such as "gender perspective," "gendering politics" or "gender mainstreaming." This might simply reflect strategic considerations, but it could also represent a genuine broadening of the perspective in order to include not only the position of women, but gender relations and gendered structures in general.

Even the concept of "gender equality" has some limitations. First, there are issues for which no male equivalent exists, for example, safe childbirth. Second, gender equality can, as seen in the Global Gender Gap Index, be measured in terms of gaps between men and women, disregarding levels: this places Rwanda as number five after the Nordic countries (in 2016). Meanwhile, others argue that gender equality as a goal cannot just mean that women and men are equally miserable! It might be for these reasons that the European Parliament committee has been named "Committee on Women's Rights and Gender Equality." Similarly, UN Women has the full title of United Nations Entity for Gender Equality and the Empowerment of Women. We shall now look more closely at the relationship between substantive and descriptive representation.

The critical mass theory

"It takes a certain number or percentage of women in politics, *a critical mass*, to make a difference." This argument is used all over the world, including in international declarations. A level of 30 or 33 percent of women in politics is often pointed to as the minimum requirement "proven by research" to be necessary for women to be able to make a difference. But is this true?

The critical mass theory is used as an argument for increasing the number of women in political assemblies. However, women politicians have themselves made use of the critical mass argument when defending themselves against the criticism – predominantly from feminist organizations – that they should have made more of a difference once elected. Research on critical mass theory finds it necessary to make a distinction between the *ability* of women to perform their tasks as politicians in specific contexts, whether feminists or not, and their *commitment* to work for gender equality and women's rights.

The critical mass theory has its origins in nuclear physics as well as in organizational studies of the importance of the size of the minority (gender or race). From a methodological point of view, however, it is difficult to distinguish the effect of the increase in numbers of the minority from other important factors, some of which might themselves have contributed to the enhanced representation of the minority. Even in the Nordic countries, the link between the high representation of women and these countries' extended welfare states is a contested issue. A useful research strategy is to compare policies in, for instance, municipalities with different levels of women's representation.

The suggestion that the more women there are in elected office the more the diversity of women politicians will increase is easier to test, though not backed up by available empirical evidence. Instead, the social composition of parliaments nowadays is becoming increasingly skewed in terms of class for both male and female representatives.

In spite of scholarly reservations, the "theory" of a critical mass is used worldwide as an argument for increasing women's representation, including in the quota debate.[9] The conclusion is that increased representation of women is important in many respects, but that there is no *automatic* effect of a certain gender proportion, say 30 or 40 percent women. Nor can we identify a specific and irreversible *turning point*. The policy effect of the increased number of women in politics depends on the context, the commitment of the politicians and their ability to overcome resistance – and not least on the positions of women and of feminists of both sexes in the hierarchies of power, that is, in leadership positions, to which we now turn.

Women in leadership positions

The uniformity of political leaders in terms of gender and class is a serious democratic problem. In the following section, the presence of women in positions of political leadership and their commitment to gender equality issues will be analyzed. The historical exclusion of women from many portfolios (horizontal segregation) is no less serious than vertical gender segregation (the hierarchies).

Is the number of women in political leadership positions actually increasing, or are their appointments just more publicized in the media, precisely because they are rare exceptions in the predominantly masculine world of politics? At the beginning of 2017, there were twelve elected women presidents and eight women prime ministers in the world. Twenty years earlier, in August 1996, the numbers were four and three, respectively, fluctuating a little from year to year. In her huge book of 2014, *Women of Power*, Torild Skard records seventy-three women presidents and prime ministers who have served in fifty-three states since the Second World War. This implies that more and more citizens have experienced having a woman as their top political representative.

Earlier, a government with a male prime minister and only male Cabinet ministers were seen as normal, as trustworthy. In 1999, less than 9 percent of Cabinet ministers around the world were women; by 2015 this had increased to 18 percent, though the increase now seems to have leveled off. Europe scores highest, followed today by sub-Saharan Africa and the Americas, but with large intra-regional variations.[10] There is a certain correspondence between women's presence in parliament and in government. However, in the Arab states and in Asia, both with strong patriarchal traditions, the percentage of women in government is lower than in parliament.[11]

The IPU lists only eight countries in the world without any women in their government in 2015, among them Bosnia-Herzegovina, Brunei, Hungary, Pakistan and Saudi Arabia. The very first women ministers, all from before 1945, have reported that they were subject to a constant probing into their qualifications. Here they are:

1918 Soviet Union: Alexandra Kollontai, Commissioner for Social Affairs
1918 Ukraine: Evgenia Bosh, Minister of Interior
1924 Denmark: Nina Bang, Minister of Education
1926 Finland: Miina Sillanpää, Minister of Social Affairs

1929 United Kingdom: Margaret Bondfield,
     Minister of Labour
1933 USA (federal): Frances Perkins, Minister of
     Labor
1936 Spain: Federica Montseny, Minister of
     Health
1938 China: Feng Yunhe, Commissioner of the
     Economics Committee
1944 Ecuador: Nelda Martinez, Minister of
     Interior

In the first years after the Second World War, several other countries, including India, Bulgaria, Sweden and Australia, got their first – but only – woman government minister.

What do the portfolios of these first female ministers tell us? Although the spectrum is broader than expected, nevertheless social affairs, labor, health and education were well represented and have remained dominant areas among the portfolios of women ministers even today. The reaction of the public is ambivalent: is this the result of the choice by female ministers to specialize in issues that are especially important to women and children, and within areas they might have previous experience from working life or local politics – or is it an effect of women being excluded from male-dominated fields? At any rate it seems unreasonable to use the term "soft" (though the term is even used in feminist research) for the portfolios of social affairs or education, especially as today these areas have some of the largest budgets, after defense.

The range of portfolios taken up by women is rapidly expanding, and now includes finance and defense, some of the last male bastions. These changes are both substantial and symbolic. It was a cultural shock to many when the first female defense minister in Spain, Carme María Chacón Piqueras, filed past a military parade in 2008 while eight months pregnant, and a picture of this event soon reached the world media.

Commitment
There have been many constraints on the first women prime ministers, because the position is masculine-coded. But differences in their personal commitment should also be taken into account. Britain's first woman prime minister, Margaret Thatcher (1979–90, Conservative), did only appoint one other woman to her Cabinet, and, while she broke the long-standing tradition of exclusively male prime ministers, paradoxically she also reinforced the patriarchal order. In contrast, the first female Norwegian prime minister, Gro Harlem Brundtland

(1981, 1986–9, 1990–96; Labor), hit front pages around the world with her second government, which comprised an almost equal number of women and men. Even if a government is a collective and its political color decisive, there are, nevertheless, numerous examples of women ministers, and some male ministers too, who have made a considerable difference in advancing women-friendly legislation through a reluctant government and parliament.

Glass ceiling and glass cliff

We are very far from parity in terms of political leadership around the world. An overwhelming number of local mayors, and most leaders within the hierarchies of parliament, are still men. We do, however, see a growing number of women as *committee chairs* and *party leaders*, positions that may very well lead to government positions. A woman *speaker* in parliament was unimaginable in most countries for a long time, but today there are more than fifty-three women speakers in one or other of the parliamentary chambers. The Inter-Parliamentary Union (IPU) regularly invites all women speakers to a Global Summit of Women Speakers of Parliament to discuss gender policies.

The term *glass ceiling* has become a frequently used metaphor for an invisible barrier that seems to put a halt to women's careers just before they reach the top level, be it in political life, business or academia. Newer research has added that women who have managed to break the glass ceiling may face an even worse *glass cliff*. The argument is that women are often recruited to leadership positions when a business is in trouble or a party is in crisis. And yet, don't most new leaders come to power after a crisis? Pamela Paxton and Melanie Hughes add that female leaders are virtually always elected through regular channels, not military coups.[12]

Is the glass ceiling being broken? In a cohort analysis of MPs elected for the first time in 1997 in the British Labour Party (the female MPs were the "Blair's Babes" mentioned earlier), Peter Allen shows that there was no statistically significant difference in the proportion of female and male MPs who later reached executive positions, nor in the gender type of the portfolio they held or the prestige of their office. Allen draws the challenging conclusion that "sex was not the driver of any pattern of executive promotion across the period studied."[13] This sounds almost too good to be true.

An alternative explanation might be that this does not reflect the utopia of gender neutrality in politics, but rather is the result of gender parity as a *deliberate* driver in the minds of the party leaders. The neo-institutionalist focus on informal norms points to changes in this context in what we might call the "acceptable minimum" of women, defined as the minimum number or share of women, which, for instance, a prime minister must appoint to the government in order to avoid a public outcry that they are letting women down. Thus changing norms about what is a fair gender distribution lie behind the increase in the acceptable minimum of women in, for instance, a government: in a European context, from one obligatory woman minister, later two to three, to today's average of 20 percent women in government. Moreover, the newly independent countries seem to have started at a higher level, in line with the new international norms. A handful of countries have 50–50 women and men in government today, including Finland, Sweden, Norway, Cape Verde, France, Liechtenstein and Canada.

We cannot, however, assume that every newly created party will share the new norms. It is part of the creed of right-wing anti-immigration parties to go against established norms and to reject what is considered "politically correct." In general, the *first generation* of anti-immigrant parties usually has male leaders, a low number of women in their parliamentary groups, and many more male than female voters. In contrast, among the *second generation* of anti-immigrant, right-wing parties, there are many female party leaders, as in Norway, France, Germany, and previously in Denmark and Australia, as well as a growing number of female MPs and a diminishing, though still considerable, gender gap among the voters. In the United States, Donald Trump's administration has only a couple of female ministers, the lowest share since the 1970s.

To sum up: it is mainly women politicians who have lifted the gender equality issue on to the political agenda, and, to a larger extent than their male colleagues, they have supported gender equality policies, and may even have managed to get the whole party to embrace them. Having scrutinized more recent empirical research on women's substantive representation, the Swedish political scientist Lena Wängnerud summarizes by stating that, even if recent empirical studies provide mixed results, taken together, "the picture that emerges shows that female politicians contribute to strengthening the position of women's interests" – that is, they are not merely symbolic representatives.[14] The policy result is what in research is labeled "state feminism."

State feminism

The term "state feminism" was originally used ironically: how can a *patriarchal* state be feminist? Since then, however, the use of this term has become commonplace to indicate public gender equality policy.

Comparative studies of gender equality policies are a relatively new research area. Instead of questioning the difference that women politicians make, this research asks which policies have been adopted in different countries or municipalities; how has gender equality policy been framed in discourse; which political conditions have proved most favorable to the adoption of gender equality policies; and how has resistance been overcome?[15]

In a comparative analysis of thirteen Western countries, Dorothy McBride, Amy Mazur and their co-authors conclude that *women's policy agencies*, for instance women's commissions or gender equality councils, have been key players, although to varying degrees according to the policy area and the context.[16] Thus behind the expanding public gender-equality policy, including anti-discrimination legislation, equal pay provisions, parental leave and day-care centers etc., there often stood a "Velvet Triangle," consisting of state actors (women's policy agencies), the women's movement and (female) legislators.[17] The next step is to scrutinize the extent to which gender equality policies have been – or not been – implemented and the effects they have had in various contexts.[18]

However, following the global introduction of *gender mainstreaming*, many women's policy agencies, later renamed gender equality units, have been closed. Gender mainstreaming was apparently a feminist dream come true – integrating a feminist perspective with all policy-making and implementation. And yet the drive behind gender-equality policy risks being lost, not least because women's movements and even female politicians have started to be dismissed as those policies have become increasingly bureaucratized. The *juridification* of gender-equality policies, familiar from the many court cases in the USA, but also from a tendency towards litigation within the European Union, changes the balance between the state, collective bargaining and the judiciary in favor of the latter, which again tends to disempower collective actors such as trade unions and parliaments, with important consequences for issues such as the pay gap and gender discrimination in the labor market.

With gender mainstreaming as today's predominant instrument for gender-equality politics, there is an obvious danger that the transformative force of the demands of the women's movements disappears. Studying government action on violence against women in seventy countries over four decades, and the fierce resistance to such measures, Mala Htun and S. Laurel Weldon conclude that ". . . policies promoting gender equality seek fundamental social change and therefore challenge historical patterns of state–society interaction concerning relations between the state and the market; the respective authority of the state, religion, and cultural groups; and the contours of citizenship."[19] Does this mean that feminists should give up on the state?

The state as ally or enemy?

Both radical and socialist feminism have – to various degrees depending on the country and the time period – expressed skepticism toward state intervention on gender-equality issues: is it really possible to change the patriarchal regime through legislation? Liberal feminism, in contrast, used to see state intervention as a possible strategy for changing male dominance in politics. Nevertheless, all strands of feminism have from time to time asked for new state interventions. "Bring the state back in," American political scientist Theda Skocpol recommended during the heated discussions in the 1980s.[20]

Following Olof Palme's line of reasoning, and speaking in systemic terms, it could be argued that women's organizations in general have a better chance of influencing the political system than of influencing the discriminatory market forces, including multinational companies, provided that a minimum number of transparent and accessible democratic institutions is in place. I will conclude that, at large, women – as individuals, as specific groups of women, for instance single mothers or trade union women, and as a group in general – need well-functioning and open democracies to secure what American feminist Nancy Fraser has labeled the recognition, redistribution and participation of women.

I will end this chapter with a list of *state interventions* needed to counteract the discriminatory effects of market forces and inequality in civil society. This list may be used as a springboard for further discussions:

- redistribution of money and resources to women, e.g. to single mothers, for maternity care and maternity leave
- actions against the feminization of poverty
- public services: care for children, the elderly and disabled

- housing and public transportation
- an independent judiciary and police without gender biases and homophobia; interventions against domestic violence; anti-discrimination regulations, i.e. on equal pay and equal treatment; and affirmative action, i.e. gender quotas
- support for men's role as caregivers, e.g. paternity leave
- protection from sexual violence and harassment in peace and in war and the inclusion of women in peace negotiations and post-conflict reconciliation.

The lesson learnt so far is that strong women's organizations, lobbyists as well as grass-roots movements, and considerable representation of women in decision-making forums, including parliaments and governments, are needed in order to adopt and implement such policies – and in order to persuade male politicians and political parties as such to support them.

We have seen significant increases in women's representation – although we are still very far from achieving parity – and a growing national institutionalization of gender-equality policies. However, at the same time, democracies are losing decision-making power to the global market and to emerging regional and global governance structures. In the final chapter we will therefore scrutinize the presence of women and of gender-equality policies at the global level. Are global governance structures even more male-dominated than national politics?

5

Women in Global Politics

Is there even more gender imbalance in global governance structures than there is in national political institutions? The answer is undoubtedly yes. This chapter analyzes some recent structural changes in global governance, of importance – directly or indirectly – for the presence of women and the inclusion of gender equality perspectives. Three cases are discussed: first, women in economic governance (especially the World Bank); then women in peace negotiations (UN Resolution 1325); and, finally, we discuss the importance of the UN system for the development of transnational feminism, asking how women's movements can be empowered in global governance. The chapter ends with some general conclusions relating to the book as a whole.

Global democracy

An increasing number of authoritative decisions are now being taken at regional and global levels. Many of the debates and referenda over new European Union treaties, and most recently the heated discussions over the Transatlantic Trade and Investment Partnership (TTIP), revolve around the balance between democratic decision-making at the national level and the power of international institutions, often influenced by multinational companies.

Academics have long disagreed on the feasibility of creating a global democracy; at the same time, regional institutions such as the EU have been criticized for decades for their "democratic deficit." While American political scientist Robert A. Dahl argued that global democracy is impossible because of the absence of a global *demos* and that, instead, international organizations should be treated as ordinary organizations from which we should require transparency and accountability, others, including David Held in his quest for "Cosmopolitan Democracy," believe that global democracy is both desirable and possible to achieve. This may be too optimistic.

Anthony Giddens has defined globalization as "the intensification of worldwide social relations which link distant localities in such a way that local happenings are shaped by events occurring many miles away and vice versa."[1] In a way, the global is nowhere and everywhere, as it consists of a web of discourses, institutions, networks and more or less opaque power structures. Globalization in terms of trade, financial transactions, knowledge spread and migration may have been more extensive in earlier periods, while other dimensions – including cultural exchange, tourism, music and discourses around new political issues such as environmental problems and gender inequality – are today spreading more widely and more rapidly than ever before. The Internet has contributed immensely to global cooperation, and has facilitated the development of transnational non-governmental organizations (TNGOs).

The study of *global governance* organizations is a growing area of research, which, however, lacks a gender perspective – with the exception of the new feminist research in the area. Global governance organizations are here defined as various systems of international cooperation that are initiated through intergovernmental agreements between states and still under the strong influence of the stakeholders, but that increasingly work independently.

Economic global governance

"The next step must be the full inclusion of women in global economic summits." This demand was made by Helen Clark, former prime minister of New Zealand, and since 2009 leader of the United Nations Development Programme (UNDP). The "family photos" taken at the countless summits following the economic crisis feature a large majority of male leaders – alongside Germany's Angela Merkel and the IMF's Christine Lagard.

Male dominance in global governance reflects the unequal gender composition of national political leadership that we saw in Chapter 4. Yet recent decades have seen some moderate gendering of, for instance, the International Monetary Fund (IMF), the World Trade Organization (WTO) and the World Bank, the world's largest development bank.

Previously, the World Bank was inaccessible to women's organizations, which it considered irrelevant to its work. That changed after strong feminist criticism in the 1980s of the bank's structural adjustment programs (SAPs), which prescribed state withdrawal from the market and severe cuts in public spending. Initially the bank established a small three-person Women in Development Office (WIP). Following criticism from women's transnational movements, including DAWN, the influential network of feminist researchers and activists from the economic South, the bank under President James Wolfensohn established a more intense dialogue with civil society, which included partnership projects.[2] Later, the bank established gender and development policy sections and research units, and formally adopted the World Bank's Gender Policies. The bank today has a high-level panel, the World Bank Advisory Council on Gender and Development.

Even the World Economic Forum, a privately organized conclave of some of the world's most powerful business and political leaders, which is held in Davos, Switzerland, has most recently, following strong feminist criticism, included gender issues in its program and developed a Global Gender Gap Index as a complement to UNDP's Gender Development Index. In 2016, 18 percent of the participants at Davos were women, reflecting, one could argue, the degree of male dominance in global politics.

Feminist scholars have criticized the neoliberal discourse used by these economic organizations around the new inclusion of women – the *utility of women* argument. Here is an example from the World Bank: "Failure to fully unleash women's productive potential represents a major missed opportunity with significant consequences for individuals, families, and economies." Feminist critics ask whether women are now "going to bed with neoliberal capitalism" and becoming an instrument of governmentality?[3] Is this a case of feminism being "co-opted"?[4]

The utility argument is the fifth and latest argument for the inclusion of women, as outlined in Chapter 1, and is fast becoming the dominant discourse in economic circles today. Women are good for business! The problem is that if the inclusion of women is not seen as a right, what happens if the presence of women does not produce improved economic results? And, again, how do we isolate the economic effect of including more women from other factors, including those factors that opened up for women in the first place?

Structural openings

Some new opportunities for women's global presence have arisen almost unnoticed as a result of recent institutional changes in global governance. First, the increase in the number of *parliamentary assemblies* connected to international organizations has opened them up to more reports and discussions on gender equality, following the growth in women's representation in national parliaments, which normally select the delegates to these international assemblies.[5] The European Parliament (now 35 percent women) is an exception, having directly elected members. At present, a third of the world's important international organizations have a parliamentary assembly, and a count of members of the NATO Parliamentary Assembly shows that it comprises 17 percent women.

Second, and probably of even greater importance, there is an increased openness on the part of international governance organizations toward *transnational non-governmental actors*, such as business, experts and civil society organizations, including transnational organizations (TNGOs) and many other stakeholders. The United Nations was among the first post-war organizations to grant access to civil society organizations, but many international organizations have followed suit – most prevalently in the areas of human rights and development, and least in the area of security. This comes partly as a response to the criticism that global governance institutions suffer from serious democratic deficits, and partly from their own interest in including experts from civil society.[6] Participation in international meetings, however, requires substantial human and financial resources, and, as a result, most participants come from the developed countries.[7] Formalized access and financial support are therefore especially important to women's TNGOs, which in general lack sufficient economic resources.

Third, a few international governance institutions have adopted *gender quotas*. Quotas are not unknown in global governance, but are mostly to be found in the mechanisms for distributing seats and voting power between participating countries. The following institutions make use of gender quotas:

Inter-Parliamentary Union (IPU) involves a unique cooperation between parliaments of the world. Currently there are 171 member parliaments and eleven associated members. National parliaments that attend three consecutive IPU assemblies without both men and women represented in their delegations have their voting rights reduced, and the total number of delegates allowed to participate is cut back by one. Voting rights in the IPU Governing Council are similarly reduced. Sanctions have actually been applied over the past few years against Haiti, Lithuania, the Federated

States of Micronesia, Qatar, Malta, Mauritius and Somalia, and, most recently, against Bulgaria, the Democratic People's Republic of Korea and again Micronesia and Qatar.[8]

African Union (AU). According to the statutes of the AU, no fewer than half of the ten members of the Commission of the AU must be women. This radical quota provision was the result of strong intervention by African women leaders at the formation of the AU in 2002. The no less than 50 percent women quota also applies to all senior, professional and technical appointments. In comparison, only 32 percent of the EU Commissioners are women.

International Criminal Court (ICC), which tries individuals for genocide, war crimes and crimes against humanity, is an international organization and an international tribunal – not to be confused with the older International Court of Justice (ICJ), which tries states. Both courts are located in The Hague. In selecting the judges, the state parties must take into account representation of "the principal legal systems of the world, equitable geographical representation and a fair representation of female and male judges, also including judges with legal expertise of special issues, including, but not limited to, violence against women or children."[9]

Women in Global Politics

Women in peace negotiations

"I recall one woman saying that 'a typical peace process involved bad men forgiving other bad men in fancy hotels in front of television cameras'!"

Mary Robinson, former president of Ireland,
speaking at the annual Desmond Tutu
International Peace Lecture,
9 October 2014

The UN Security Council Resolution 1325 (SCR 1325) of 2000 on Women, Peace and Security was a landmark in two respects: first, by stating that women and children are particularly affected by armed conflicts; and, second, by stressing the importance of including women in conflict prevention and resolution. It was followed by seven complementary resolutions. Here are extracts from the preamble to SCR 1325.

The Security Council . . . Expressing concern that civilians, particularly women and children, account for the vast majority of those adversely affected by armed conflict, including as refugees and internally displaced persons, and increasingly are targeted by combatants and armed elements, and *recognizing* the consequent impact this has on durable peace and reconciliation.

Reaffirming the important role of women in the prevention and resolution of conflicts and in peace-building, and *stressing* the importance of their equal participation and full involvement in all efforts for the maintenance and promotion of peace and security, and the need to increase their role in decision-making with regard to conflict prevention and resolution.

Does this constitute a quota provision? "Equal participation" and "full involvement" are familiar goals from the quota debate, but the rules here are not clearly spelt out and there are no sanctions for non-compliance. By 2016, however, fifty-five UN member states and some regional organizations, including the African Union, the European Union and the Pacific Islands Forum, had adopted the required National Action Plans.

Northern Ireland.
"In 1996, the negotiators of the Northern Ireland Good Friday Agreement (GFA) invited the top ten political parties to the negotiating table. None of them had female representation. When they realized this, Monica McWilliams [Catholic] and May Blood [Protestant] formed the Northern Ireland Women's Coalition (NIWC) and managed

to secure the 10,000 signatures required to form a political party, thus gaining a seat for women at the negotiation table. . . . The NIWC . . . built bridges between the Protestant and Catholic communities, and they believed that the ownership of the terms of any agreement should not be solely in the hands of those sitting around the table . . . The NIWC were highly involved in the drafting of the GFA and had a strong popular mandate." (From the report Making Women Count – Not Just Counting Women: Assessing Women's Inclusion and Influence on Peace Negotiations, Inclusive Peace & Transition Initiative and UN Women, April 2016)

The first results of SCR 1325, if measured alone in terms of figures on women's presence, are meagre. At the most recent peace negotiations, less than 8 percent of the participants and less than 3 percent of the signatories have been women. Even so, Mary Robinson became the first female UN Special Envoy when she led a peacekeeping delegation to the Great Lakes Region of Africa in 2013. After the adoption of SCR 1325, peace agreements, especially in Africa, had begun to incorporate the language of women's rights as a result of domestic and international pressure.[10]

The report *Making Women Count – Not Just Counting Women* quoted above is one of the most comprehensive evaluations, based on forty cases and covering thirty-four countries from 1989 to 2014. Seven types (modalities) of inclusion of women's groups or coalitions are identified: (1) Direct representation at the negotiation table; (2) Observer status; (3) Consultations; (4) Inclusive commissions; (5) High-level problem-solving workshops; (6) Public decision-making, e.g. referenda; and (7) Mass action (pp. 36–7):

> Our research shows that, in most cases with strong women's involvement (15 out of 40), women specifically and successfully pushed for and supported the peace process. In particular, women's participation through modalities 1 (direct representation), 2 (observer status), and 7 (mass action) seem to provide the most favorable entry points for their pro-peace activities. . . . For example, in the **DRC** (modality 1), the 40 female delegates in Sun City ensured that the agreement was signed by forming a human chain to block the exits to the committee room. They insisted that the men would not leave until the signing of the agreement. In the 1993 Conference of National Reconciliation in **Somalia**, some of the women observers (modality 2) at the conference decided to publicly pressure faction

leaders by fasting until an agreement was reached. The men produced a peace plan 24 hours later. In **Somaliland** during the post-independence violence negotiations (1991–1994), women's groups with observer status (modality 2) were highly influential in forcing the conflict parties to the table, and in keeping them there until concrete progress had been made. They also acted as de facto mediators and communicators. Because they were widely perceived as being more impartial than male colleagues, this trust allowed these observers to help facilitate the smooth progress of negotiations. Similarly, in **Liberia** and **Somaliland** (modality 7), women outside the negotiation venue pressured the men to sign the agreement by threatening to publically undress themselves in full view of the negotiators. For a son to see his mother naked is especially inappropriate in that cultural context, and these women used and instrumentalized status quo gendered roles to advocate for peace. While these cases illustrate possibilities entailing direct physical proximity and access to negotiation venues, the case of **Northern Ireland** shows how women can also successfully mobilize for peace through a mass campaign (modality 7) that is much broader and all-encompassing in scope.

The *Making Women Count* report concludes that women have made substantial contributions to peace-making and constitution-building, even though the inclusion of women is still challenged or met with indifference by many negotiating parties and mediators. In general, women were found to be most influential when they pushed for concrete reforms, including gender-sensitive provisions in the new constitutions, as was the case in Rwanda. Early inclusion of women, preferably in the pre-negotiation phase, has often paved the way for sustained inclusion throughout the process.

The most often cited part of the report is the conclusion that "the strength of women's influence is positively correlated with agreements being reached and implemented" (p. 6). Does this means "the more women, the more peace?" The report wisely speaks of correlations, not causality. But other researchers have also pointed out that the inclusion of representatives of civil society, such as women's organizations, has helped and has bestowed greater legitimacy on the peace process and decreased the risk of a return to conflict.[11]

The conclusion is that women are strongest when united across ethnic and religious divides.[12] As an expert on gender quotas, I was invited to a women's meeting in Sarajevo on 23 March 1999 – the day before NATO starting bombing Serbia – and I witnessed the formation of a fragile coalition of women from all three groups in the ongoing conflict, united behind a demand for gender quotas in parliament, which eventually became permanent.

Armed conflicts and political transition processes tend to disrupt traditional gender roles and structures. Rwanda is thus not an exception but rather is representative of many post-conflict countries that have adopted electoral gender quotas as part of the reconciliation process and transition from authoritarian regimes.[13] These results make SCR 1325 even more important.

Are women more peaceful than men?

Even if most researchers see SCR 1325 as breaking new normative ground in its Women, Peace and Security agenda, many express disappointment with the lack of change in general perceptions of militarism, war and peace. Is this just an attempt at "making war safe for women" rather than a challenge to the gendered impacts of militarism? Are the Action Plans primarily used as "markers" of civilizational advancement, for instance in the case of NATO? Is SCR 1325 "essentializing" women? Some further criticize the Women, Peace and Security agenda for being imperialistic, whereas others point to the energetic participation of the Global South in the process of its formation.[14]

Scrutinizing the text of 1325 provides no clues. Maybe for strategic reasons, no explanations are given for the need to include women at all stages – from conflict prevention over conflict resolution to peace-building. There is no reference to women's presence as a right or to the benefit of including women's experiences as caregivers or to any conflicts of interests between women and men in war. The newer democracy argument and utility argument are also absent.

The criticism of SCR 1325 represents a recurring point of conflict within feminist theory about "essentialism." A parallel debate has emerged over the finding that countries with higher women's representation are also the countries with the lowest levels of corruption.[15]

However, to take the point of departure from women's actual experiences and competences is not to make a biological argument or to "essentialize" women, unless one assumes that men could not acquire the same experiences and skills in similar contexts. Further, the fact that not all women work as caregivers and that some women are corrupt does not make care or corruption less gendered.

Yet some women's groups have successfully made use of traditional gender roles. To the example from Somaliland cited above, one can add the Argentine

Madres de la Plaza de Mayo, who walked around and around the square demanding information about their children who went missing during the dictatorship regime, or the Committee of Soldiers' Mothers in Russia. These examples contribute to the discussion of the kind of power women can mobilize in order to effect change.

The influence of transnational women's organizations

What opportunities exist for women's transnational non-governmental organizations to influence the global agenda and decision-making? International cooperation between women's organizations is, as we have seen, nothing new. Their influence has two aspects: first, they act directly on the international scene in attempting to influence global and regional governance organizations and institutions; second, they provide support and legitimacy to national and local initiatives, as we have seen in the previous chapters.

The number of transnational women's organizations has increased, especially following the UN world conferences. Some take the form of umbrella structures for national women's organizations, the European Women's Lobby; others have been established from the beginning as international organizations, for example, DAWN. *The Oxford Handbook of Transnational Feminist Movements*, published in 2015, provides an excellent overview of the work of TNGOs within various sectors such as health and body politics, human rights, economic and social justice, and feminist political ecology.[16]

While TNGOs have criticized the lack of representativeness of international organizations, other critics have questioned who the TNGOs themselves represent? The professionalization needed to make it on the regional and international scene often creates a gap between the TNGOs and domestic grass-roots organizations, which have few resources other than the commitment of the participants. The grass-roots organizations are no doubt the losers, when decision-making turns regional or global. Nevertheless, the Internet has made a tremendous difference, increasing the speed and reducing the high costs of international cooperation. Yet the costs of international activism may be too great for younger people and those with fewer resources, and the effects of traditional demonstrations are, unfortunately, too small – unless they turn violent.[17]

Global feminism(s)

It makes sense to speak about global feminism both in the singular – stressing the common ideas of the movements – and in the plural.[18] Many women's TNGOs, including trade union networks and large religious networks, may not identify themselves as feminist movements, here defined as movements resisting the whole patriarchal order, but they may nonetheless engage in broad coalitions of women's organizations on special issues, for example on equal pay, combating sexual violence against women and girls, women's representation, girls' education and improvements in maternity care. It is remarkable that there are so few, if any, *transnational anti-feminist* women's organizations (such movements mostly have male leaders).

That feminism is principally a Western trend is a recurring argument, frequently expressed by anti-feminists in the Global South. It is true that levels of feminist mobilization fluctuate in different parts of the world at different times.[19] Academics Mina Roces and Louise Edwards argue that, after having associated the word "feminism" with Western feminism for much of the twentieth century, Asian women activists gradually changed their perception, not least after women from all over the world discussed women's rights together at the UN World

Congresses.[20] Also referring to the UN, British sociologist Sylvia Walby prefers the more modest "transnational feminism" to the concept "global feminism" – except when talking about interventions at the level of the United Nations.[21]

The role of the UN

The United Nations and its agencies have become the most important international arena for women's growing global presence and for developing new global gender discourses – "a catalyst for feminist strategizing internationally."[22] The spring meeting of the Commission on the Status of Women (CSW) is a lively venue for interchanges between government representatives, parliamentarians and women's NGOs and TNGOs. Further, the Convention on the Elimination of All Forms of Discrimination against Women (CEDAW), instituted in 1981, represents another important platform, since individual states are obliged to report their progress on gender equality to the CEDAW Commission, while the national women's rights organizations have the opportunity to publish critical shadow reports.[23]

Today, almost all UN agencies have gender equality units, officers and projects. In addition to its own multitude of projects, UN Women has a role as watchdog in relation to other UN agencies: this is an important role, though not always popular within the UN system! The four UN World Conferences on Women – in Mexico (1975), Copenhagen (1980), Nairobi (1985) and Beijing (1995) – were extremely important for the expansion of transnational women's networks, not least through the parallel NGO conferences. Moreover, one should not underestimate the importance of the locations of these UN conferences for the development of regional women's networks. All in all, the UN – and especially UN Women's role in the empowerment of women – is a good example of what is known as the "UN as a normative power."

Discursive power

What kind of power do national and transnational women's movements possess to open up national, regional and global governance structures? *The Oxford Handbook of Transnational Feminist Movements* rightly stresses the development of knowledge, policy and social change.[24] I would, in addition, conclude that the strongest asset of the women's movements, nationally and internationally, is their power to change social discourses through *mobilizing new ways of thinking and new norms and practices* – and to spread them through large international networks with considerable effects on political decision-making. We have also seen that when women's organizations have formed broad coalitions, their influence has increased considerably – because in such cases they have access to all parties and to almost all levels of society, as there are women in all "camps."

Here are some important examples of such discursive changes. In cooperation with *gender experts* in the academic world – with the many *femocrats* working from within, as well as with *feminist politicians (of both genders)* – women's movements have been the main actors behind many important discursive transformations: changing the gender blindness of developmental politics; the inclusion of reproductive health in population policy; the inclusion of a gender perspective in peace negotiations and peace-making; the inclusion of domestic workers under International Labor Organization (ILO) regulations; achieving the recognition of rainbow families in World Bank family projects; drawing attention to gender issues within the climate change discourse; raising issues of sexual violence against women and girls during armed conflicts, even by UN peace-keeping forces, which has become a matter for international justice (as crimes against humanity) – and so much more. All of this, however, does not yet add up to the ultimate goal set by UN Women's Executive Director,

South African Phumzile Mlambo-Ngcuka, namely that of "dismantling patriarchy."

Conclusion

This book started with optimism about the empowerment of women in politics, as expressed during and after the Beijing conference of 1995. In concluding this book, it must, however, be said that this sense of optimism seems less prevalent today, maybe especially in the old democracies. One indicator of this is the decision not to organize a Beijing+20 World Conference on women in 2015. Due to the current strength of religious and political fundamentalism in many regions of the world, it was feared that the important gains of the Beijing declaration, Platform for Action, could be lost.[25]

One may ask, are we still on the track towards gender equality in politics? What are the prospects of achieving, before the target year of 2030, one of the UN's new Sustainable Development Goals (SDG), namely to "Ensure women's full and effective participation and equal opportunities for leadership at all levels of decision-making in politics, economics and public life" (SDG 5.5)? This schedule may prove to be too ambitious.

This book has described how democracy has failed women from its very beginnings. The exclusion without words was the most devastating, as discussed in Chapter 1. Different dimensions of male dominance in politics were presented in Chapter 2, and have been discussed throughout the book: the under-representation of women in elected assemblies and in political leadership; the horizontal gender segregation of portfolios, male-coded norms and practices; the gendered perceptions of politicians, and a limited concern for gender equality, which has not been a salient or prioritized issue in electoral campaigns or government platforms almost anywhere. In numerical terms, the political arena is still grossly male-dominated. Politics is still failing women, yet there is a lot to learn from the last two decades' obvious progress.

That women have a place in politics today is indisputable. The traditionalists, who want to push women back to the home, have a lost cause. Many cultural barriers have been overcome. Global South countries, through the use of fast-track policies such as gender quotas, are challenging the old democracies' incremental policies.

Today, an all-male assembly or government has in most parts of the world lost its democratic legitimacy, and the "acceptable minimum" of women has increased. The goal of gender balance has been adopted in international declarations and by civil society organizations as expressed by the Namibian Women's Manifesto Network: "50–50. Women and men in government – get the balance right!" Even if blaming women for their under-representation is still widespread, there is a shift – which I have witnessed as an advisor on women's empowerment in politics around the world – towards a sharper focus on the lack of inclusiveness on the part of political institutions, including political parties, which, in spite of being the real gatekeepers to elected positions, are rarely addressed specifically in international declarations.

Increased global transparency has paved the way for competition amongst countries, and a high level of women's representation has become a symbol of "democracy" and being "modern," which women's rights advocates have been able to use in their campaigns.

However, the "stickiness" of male dominance in political institutions has meant that it has been left to women and to other newcomers in politics to adapt to existing political norms and practices. Electoral gender quotas represent one of the first substantial structural reforms, a change in the "how" of political procedures in order to broaden the "who" of policy-making to include women – and, in the future, hopefully also minorities and immigrants. This book has shown that in over half the countries of the world some type of electoral gender quotas are in use today. Gender quotas, however, are no miracle cure for women's lack of campaign financing or intimidation during campaigns, for example. But properly designed electoral gender quotas are an effective equality measure against the "old boys' network," even if mixed motives lie behind their adoption. A valuable lesson has been learnt that sustainable and effective gender quotas depend on the mobilization of women's organizations and networks, prior to, during and after the adoption of such quotas. In general, every improvement in women's representation and every quota adoption has been the result of intervention by women's movements and women's rights advocates.

The theory of shrinking institutions, with its two contrasting versions – "women in, then power out" or "power out, then women in" – cannot be substantiated. But national parliaments and local councils are today being challenged by structural changes in society, which shift decision-making powers to regional and global governance institutions and to multinational companies – also to

144

independent companies as a result of political decisions to privatize or outsource tasks that were previously seen as common public services, such as the postal service, hospitals, train networks or energy supplies.

The contested Norwegian quota law demanding at least 40 percent women as well as men on public and private company boards was partly a response to the privatization of previously public companies with many women in their leadership. This has been followed by similar laws passed in Spain, Iceland, Belgium, France, Germany, India, Israel and Italy, with more to come. The conclusion is that it is extremely important that major structural changes are scrutinized from a gender perspective. This should also be seen as a responsibility for the growing number of women in leadership positions today, and for feminists of all genders.

This book has also discussed the opposition in some parts of the feminist movement to having more women in the established political institutions, many of which are in crisis today. There is no doubt a need for thorough discussions about the potential and the limits of this strategy. Evidently it would be naive to believe that patriarchal structures at large can be changed by political means alone, without fundamental changes in civil society and the market. However, it is argued here that, based on the way in which free market forces discriminate against women, and given the patriarchal practices deeply rooted in many types of civil society, women from all walks of life around the globe need inclusive democracies and transparent and accountable public institutions to combat violence against women and to secure women's rights and gender equality.

In contrast to previous eras, women's parliamentary representation today is almost the same in democratic regimes as in semi-democratic or authoritarian regimes. As this book has shown, this is the result not least of the adoption of electoral gender quotas by all types of political regimes, especially by those in post-conflict countries, which, as research has shown, has offered opportunities for the dislocation of some of the old male political elites, especially in Africa. In general, we find a re-evaluation among researchers today of the importance of the mobilization of women for the emergence of new democratic regimes, as well as in the histories of old democracies.

As we have seen, global governance is undoubtedly more gender-imbalanced than national decision-making, yet global governance institutions do offer some new opportunities for women's rights advocates and transnational women's movements. After all, global governance is necessary for the survival of the globe. Even if David Held's global democracy might be impossible, reforming global governance institutions, including the United Nations, is of the utmost importance. Global governance is unquestionably preferable to decision-making by a few world leaders with close links to multinational companies. With recent shifts in world leadership, this latter scenario may well become more prevalent.

Since the likelihood of adopting gender-equality policies is so much higher when women – including a diversity of women – are present, the politics of gender parity in political institutions is essential for the elimination of all discrimination against women, as well as for the revitalization of democracies. Apart from sometimes significant policy effects, changing the historical male monopoly over political decision-making should be considered a social transformation in its own right.

It would, however, be a mistake to think that the present move from a small to a large minority of women in politics implies that gender parity will be attained automatically and that we will not see any backlash. Rather, we might in the future see increasing clashes between anti-feminists and women's rights advocates. One lesson from history is that advances in women's empowerment and gender equality do not follow a pre-written script but instead depend on a multiplicity of factors and always require hard work on the part of women's movements throughout the world.

Further Reading and Resources

The film *Suffragette* (2015) is an excellent introduction to actions, arguments and counter-arguments during one of the most militant campaigns for women's suffrage, that of the British movement. Most new empirical research on the fight for suffrage, often undertaken because of recent or upcoming centenaries for women's suffrage, is published, for good reason, in the language of the respective countries; but there are nevertheless some new comprehensive studies available in English: e.g. Irma Sulkunen et al., *Suffrage, Gender and Citizenship: International Perspectives on Parliamentary Reforms* (Cambridge Scholars Publishing, 2009).

For studies within Feminist Theory, dealt with in Chapter1 on women's exclusion/inclusion in democratic politics, see Carole Pateman, *The Disorder of Women* (Polity Press, 1989); several works of Anne Phillips: *The Politics of Presence* (Oxford University Press, 1995), *Engendering Democracy* (Pennsylvania State University Press, 1991) and *Democracy and Difference* (John Wiley

& Sons, 2013), and Birte Siim, *Gender and Citizenship. Politics and Agency in France, Britain and Denmark* (Cambridge University Press, 2000). See also Michael Saward, *The Representative Claim* (Polity Press, 2010).

Until some decades ago, there were few studies of women's political representation (Chapter 2), but today this is a large and constantly expanding research field. The classic work is Joni Lovenduski and Pippa Norris, *Gender and Party Politics* (Sage, 1993); among the newer titles are Drude Dahlerup and Monique Leyenaar (eds), *Breaking Male Dominance in Old Democracies* (Oxford University Press, 2013); Miki Caul Kittilson and Leslie A. Schwindt-Bayer, *The Gendered Effects of Electoral Institutions* (Oxford University Press, 2012); Barbara Pini and Paula McDonald (eds), *Women and Representation in Local Government* (Routledge, 2011); Kirsti Niskanen (ed.), *Gender and Power in the Nordic Countries* (Nordic Council of Ministers, 2011); Valentine Moghadam (ed.), *From Patriarchy to Empowerment: Women's Participation, Movements, and Rights in the Middle East, North Africa, and South Asia* (Syracuse University Press, 2007) and Joni Lovenduski (ed.), *State Feminism and Political Representation* (Cambridge University Press, 2005). The first book to develop a neo-institutionalist perspective on gender and politics was Mona Lena Krook and Fiona Mackay (eds), *Gender, Politics and Institutions. Towards a Feminist Institutionalism* (Palgrave Macmillan, 2012).

If you just have a couple of hours for additional reading on this subject, I recommend Mona Lena Krook, "Why Are Fewer Women than Men Elected? Gender and Dynamics of Candidate Selection," *Political Studies Review*, 8 (2): 155–68, Wiley Online Library.

Gender quotas in politics are a new, controversial, yet widespread contemporary electoral reform (Chapter3). The growing amount of quota research often applies a comparative perspective. The first collection was Drude Dahlerup (ed.), *Women, Quotas and Politics* (Routledge, 2006), with contributions from all major regions in the world. See also Susan Franceschet, Mona Lena Krook and Jennifer M. Piscopo (eds), *The Impact of Gender Quotas* (Oxford University Press, 2012), with articles on, for example, Argentina, Rwanda and Morocco; Mala Htun, *Inclusion without Representation in Latin America. Gender Quotas and Ethnic Reservations* (Cambridge University Press, 2016); see also the special issue of the journal *Teorija in Praksa* (in English) on the effectiveness and legitimacy of gender quotas in Central and Eastern Europe (2, 2017).

For further readings on transitions to democracy seen from a gender perspective, which is discussed in Chapters 1, 2 and 3, see Georgina Waylen, *Engendering Transitions. Women's Mobilization, Institutions, and Gender Outcomes* (Oxford University Press, 2007), and Aili Mari Tripp, *Women and Power in Postconflict Africa* (Cambridge University Press, 2015).

On the intensive feminist discussion on the "substantive representation" of women, "women's interests" and the critical mass theory (Chapter 4), see Maria C. Escobar-Lemmon and Michelle M. Taylor-Robinson (eds), *Representation. The Case of Women* (Oxford University Press, 2014); Drude Dahlerup, "The Critical

Mass Theory in Public and Scholarly Debates," in Rosie Campbell and Sarah Childs (eds), *Deeds and Words. Gendering Politics after Joni Lovenduski* (ECPR Press, Colchester, 2014, pp. 137–63); and Karen Celis and Sarah Childs (eds), *Gender, Conservatism and Political Representation* (ECPR Press, 2014). See also Nira Yuval-Davis, *The Politics of Belonging. Intersectional Contestations* (Sage, 2011). Lena Wängnerud (2009) has written an excellent overview: "Women in Parliaments: Descriptive and Substantive Representation," *Annual Review of Political Science*, 21 (1): 51–69.

The (slow) growth of women in the political leadership positions (Chapter 4) has produced new comparative research; see Torild Skard's huge book, which contains interesting interviews with women world leaders: *Women of Power. Half a century of female presidents and prime ministers worldwide* (Policy Press, 2014); and Gretchen Bauer and Manon Tremblay (eds), *Women in Executive Power. A Global Overview* (Routledge, 2011). For an interesting shorter text, see Diana Z. O'Brian et al. (2015), "Letting down the Ladder or Shutting the Door: Female Prime Ministers, Party Leaders and Cabinet Ministers," *Politics & Gender*, 11 (4): 689–717.

For further reading to Chapter 4's section on "State Feminism" – the relationship between women's movements and the state – the two classic works are Helga Hernes, *Welfare State and Woman Power: essays in state feminism* (Norwegian University Press, 1987), and Vicky Randall and Georgina Waylen (eds), *Gender, Politics and the State* (Routledge, 1998, 2002). Contemporary large research projects have produced new knowledge on the

Further Reading and Resources

subject, including Dorothy McBride and Amy Mazur (eds), *The Politics of State Feminism* (RNGS-project, Temple University Press, 2010); Emanuela Lombardo, Petra Meier and Mieke Verloo (eds), *The Discursive Politics of Gender Equality* (QUING-Project, Routledge, 2009); Beatrice Halsaa, Sasha Roseneil and Sivil Sümer (eds), *Remaking Citizenship in Multicultural Europe. Women's Movements, Gender and Diversity* (FEMCIT-project, Palgrave Macmillan, 2012); Diane Sainsbury's interesting books from 1994, 1996 and 1999 on gender and welfare state regimes, and finally Sylvia Walby et al., *The Concept and Measurement of Violence Against Women and Men* (Policy Press, 2017).

Women in global politics, Chapter 5: for an overview of transnational movements and issues, see Rawwida Baksh and Wendy Harcourt (eds), *The Oxford Handbook of Transnational Feminist Movements* (Oxford University Press, 2015). As well as the many books mentioned in the Notes, see also Mina Roces and Louise Edwards (eds), *Women's Movements in Asia. Feminisms and Transnational Activism* (Routledge, 2010); Anne Sisson Runyan and V. Spike Peterson, *Global Gender Issues in the New Millennium* (Westview Press, 4th edn 2014). I also recommend Donatella de la Porta et al., *Globalization from below. Transnational Activists and Protest Networks* (University of Minnesota Press, 2006).

Finally, a useful book for further reading on key concepts and themes is Georgina Waylen et al. (eds), *The Oxford Handbook of Gender and Politics* (Oxford University Press, 2013).

Further Reading and Resources

Websites

http://www.ipu.org/wmn-e/world.htm (in English and French): women's representation in all parliaments of the world in rank order, including a month-by-month archive since 1997. Operated by the Inter-Parliamentary Union, IPU.

http://www.quotaproject.org (in English, French and Spanish): electoral gender quota systems in use throughout the world, country by country. Operated by International Idea in corporation with Stockholm University and IPU.

Key journals
Politics and Gender
Journal of Women, Politics and Policy
International Feminist Journal of Politics
European Journal of Politics and Gender – will be out in 2018

Gender equality indexes
Global Gender Gap Index (World Economic Forum)
Gender Development Index (UNDP)

Key democracy indexes
Freedom House, http://freedomhouse.org/report/freedom-world
The Economist Intelligence Unit's Democracy Index, https://infographics.economist.com/2017/DemocracyIndex
The Polity IV Index, www.systemicpeace.org/polity/polity4.htm

Further Reading and Resources

Varieties of Democracy since 1900 (V-Dem project, Gothenburg University); at https://www.v-dem.net/en (also in French, Spanish, Russian and Arabic).

Notes

Chapter 1 Exclusion Without Words

1 Michael Sawer (2010), *The Representative Claim*, Oxford University Press; Karen Celis, Sarah Child, Johanna Kantola and Mona Lena Krook (2008), "Rethinking Women's Substantive Representation," *Representation*, 44 (2), pp. 99–110.
2 Note that while man/*homme* in English and French means both a male person and human beings in general, most other languages do not confuse the two.
3 The archive of the oldest feminist organization in Denmark, Dansk Kvindesamfund (founded in 1871). The Danish Constitution of 1849 had given voting rights to a relatively broad group of men (72 percent).
4 Carole Pateman (1989), *The Disorder of Women*, Polity Press; see also Birte Siim (2000), *Gender and Citizenship. Politics and Agency in France, Britain and Denmark*, Cambridge University Press.
5 Heidi Hartmann (1979), "The unhappy marriage

between feminism and Marxism. Towards a more progressive union," *Capital & Class*, 12 (2), pp. 1–33.

6 "Suffragists" is the term used for all those working for women's enfranchisement, while "suffragettes" is the specific name for the British militant activists working for women's voting rights in the Women's Social and Political Union, but the latter term is also used to refer to the smaller group of American militants, such as those around Alice Paul's National Women's Party.

7 See Clara Zetkin's speech to the Congress of the 2nd International, Stuttgart, 1907, pp. 34–58 in Clara Zetkin (1957–60), *Ausgewählte Reden und Schriften*, Dietz Verlag, Berlin.

8 Aileen Kraditor (1965), *The Ideas of the Woman Suffrage Movement, 1890–1920*, Columbia University Press, New York; Richard J. Evans (1977), *The Feminists*, Croom Helm; Drude Dahlerup (1979), "Women's Entry into Politics," *Scandinavian Political Studies*, I (2–3), pp. 139–62.

9 J. S. Mill himself in a letter to Auguste Comte, in which they discussed – and disagreed on – the role of women in society, wrote: "there are few questions I have pondered over more." ("Il y a peu des questions que j'aie plus méditées"): *Lettres inédites de John Stuart Mill à Auguste Comte*, Édition Lévy-Brugl, Paris, 1899, p. 271 (30 Oct. 1843).

10 Pamela Paxton (2008), "Gendering Democracy," in Gary Goertz and Amy G. Mazur (eds), *Politics, Gender, and Concepts*, Cambridge University Press.

11 *No Democratic Transition Without Women's Rights: A Global Sequence Analysis 1900–2012*, V-Dem working paper 2015, University of Gothenburg; available at www.v-dem.net.

Chapter 2 Breaking Male Dominance in Politics

1 Joni Lovenduski (2005), "Introduction," in Lovenduski (ed.), *State Feminism and Political Representation*, Cambridge University Press, p. 1.
2 Interview, cited in Anthony King and Anne Sloman (1973), *Westminster and Beyond*, Macmillan, p. 55.
3 Frank C. Thames and Margaret S. Williams (2013), *Contagious Representation. Women's Political Representation in Democracies around the World*, New York University Press. Originally, this concept was used by Richard Matland and Donley T. Studlar (see n. 5 below).
4 *Atlas of Electoral Gender Quotas*, published by International IDEA, 2013, p. 23.
5 Miki Caul Kittilson and Leslie A. Schwindt-Bayer (2012), *The Gendered Effects of Electoral Institutions*, Oxford University Press; Gregory D. Schmidt (2008), "The election of women in list PR systems: Testing the conventional wisdom," *Electoral Studies*, 28 (2), pp. 190–203; Richard Matland and D.T. Studlar (2002), "Electoral systems and women's representation," *Representation*, 39 (1), pp. 3–14.
6 Anne Maria Holli and Hanna Wass (2010), "Gender-based voting in the parliamentary elections of 2007

in Finland", *European Journal of Political Research*, 49, pp. 598–630.

7 Joni Lovenduski and Pippa Norris (1993), *Gender and Party Politics*, Sage; Miki Caul Kittilson (2013), "Party Politics," in Georgina Waylen, Karen Celis, Johanna Kantola and S. Laurel Weldon (eds), *The Oxford Handbook of Gender Politics*, Oxford University Press; Karen Celis, Sarah Childs and Johanna Kantola (eds), (2016), Special issue of *Party Politics*, 22 (5).

8 Australia: the 2016 election; Sweden, 2014 election; UK, 2015 election; Germany, 2013 election.

9 Karen Celis and Sarah Childs (eds) (2014), *Gender, Conservatism and Political Representation*, ECPR Press, Colchester.

10 Per Gahrton (2015), *Green Parties, Green Future*, Pluto Press, London. The statutes of the German Greens require in present society "zumindest eine Frau" ("at least one woman") among the two spokespersons, thus allowing for two women, but not for two men.

11 Lovenduski and Norris (1993), *Gender and Party Politics*.

12 Drude Dahlerup and Lenita Freidenvall (2005), "Quotas as a 'Fast Track' to Equal Political Representation for Women. Why Scandinavia is No Longer the Model," *International Feminist Journal of Politics*, 7 (1), pp. 26–48.

13 Freedom House's index is based on the aggregate scores for countries on the basis of ten political rights and fifteen civil liberties, while *The Economist*

Intelligence Unit's index is based on broader and more demanding criteria: electoral process and pluralism, the functioning of government, political participation, political culture and civil liberties. Consequently, there are only twenty, mostly Western, countries among *The Economist*'s "full democracies," while the Freedom House index classifies 40 percent of all countries as "free" countries, implying a lower representation of women on average.

14 Pamela Paxton, Melanie M. Hughes and Matthew Painter (2010), "The Difference Time Makes: Latent Growth Curve Models of Women's Political Representation," *European Journal of Political Research*, 49 (1), pp. 25–52.

15 Melanie Hughes and Aili Mari Tripp (2015), "Civil War and Trajectories of Change in Women's Political Representation in Africa, 1985–2010," *Social Forces*, 93 (4), pp. 1513–40; see also Aili Mari Tripp (2015), *Women and Power in Postconflict Africa*, Cambridge University Press. See also Georgina Waylen (2007), *Engendering Transitions*, Oxford University Press.

16 Richard E. Matland and Kathleen A. Montgomery (eds) (2003), *Women's Access to Political Power in Post-Communist Europe*, Oxford University Press; Milica Antic and Sonja Lokar (2006), "The Balkans. From total rejection to gradual acceptance of gender quotas," in Drude Dahlerup (ed.), *Women, Quotas and Politics*, Routledge, pp. 138–67; Georgina Waylen (2007), *Engendering Transitions*, Oxford University Press.

17 Hege Skjeie (1991), "The rhetoric of difference: On women's inclusion into political elites," *Politics and Society*, 2, pp. 233–63.

Chapter 3 The Impact of Gender Quotas

1 The terms "electoral gender quotas" or "gender quotas in electoral systems" are used to distinguish gender quotas used in elections to political assemblies from quotas for internal party organizations or for company boards, even those are hot issues.

2 See the global website www.quotaprojects.org and *Atlas of Electoral Gender Quotas*, 2013–14, published by International IDEA, Stockholm University, and the Inter-Parliamentary Union (IPU). In some countries with legislated gender quotas, some of the political parties still have party quotas, perhaps even higher than the minimum required by law. These countries are here included under legislated quotas.

3 Denmark (which is no longer among the top countries with its 37 percent women in parliament), like Finland, makes no use of quotas, yet a few parties to the left made use of limited party quotas for a short period in the 1980s and early 1990s.

4 Hanane Darhour and Drude Dahlerup (2013), "Sustainable representation of women through gender quotas: A decade's experience in Morocco," *Women's Studies International Forum*, 41 (2), pp. 132–42.

5 Carol Bacchi, "Arguing for and against quotas," pp. 32–51 in Dahlerup (ed.) (2006), *Women, Quotas and*

Politics, Routledge. See also Carol Bacchi (1999), *Women, Policy and Politics*, Sage.

6 From Drude Dahlerup and Lenita Freidenvall (2010), "Judging gender quotas: predictions and results," *Policy & Politics*, 38, pp. 407–25 (slightly revised).

7 Jennie Burnet (2012), "Women's Empowerment and Cultural Change in Rwanda," in Susan Franceschet, Mona Lena Krook and Jennifer M. Piscopo (eds) (2012), *The Impact of Gender Quotas*, Oxford University Press, pp. 190–207.

8 "Gender and Political Backgrounds in Argentina," in Franceschet, Krook and Piscopo (eds) (2012), *The Impact of Gender Quotas*, pp. 27–42.

9 Rainbow Murray (2014), "Quotas for Men: Reframing Gender Quotas as a Means of Improving Representation for All," *American Political Science Review*, 108 (3), pp. 520–32.

10 Anne Phillips (1995), *The Politics of Presence*, Clarendon Press; see also Anne Phillips (2007), *Multiculturalism without culture*, Princeton University Press.

11 Monica Thresfall, Lenita Freidenvall, Malgorzata Fuszara and Drude Dahlerup (2012), "Remaking Political Citizenship in Multicultural Europe: Addressing Citizenship Deficits in the Formal Political Representation System," in Beatrice Halsaa et al. (eds), *Remaking Citizenship in Multicultural Europe*. Palgrave Macmillan, pp. 141–65.

12 The following analysis is based on Pippa Norris and Drude Dahlerup (2015), "On the Fast Track: The Spread of Gender Quota Policies for Elected

Office." First presented at the American Political Science Association Annual Meeting 2014, available in a revised form at Harvard, Kennedy School, working paper RWP 15-041, July 2015. This analysis is based on a new database, the Gender Quota Database (GQD), Stockholm University, covering 196 countries, released May 2014.

13 Freidenvall et al., in Dahlerup (ed.) (2006), *Women, Quotas and Politics*. See also the chapters on Denmark, Iceland and Sweden in Dahlerup and Leyenaar (eds), *Breaking Male Dominance in Old Democracies*.

14 Franceschet, Krook and Piscopo (eds) (2012) in *The Impact of Gender Quotas*; Adriana Piatti-Crocker (ed.) (2011), *Diffusion of Gender Quotas in Latin America and Beyond*, Peter Lang Publishers.

15 Based on the website of International IDEA, and run together with Stockholm University and the Inter-Parliamentary Union; available in English, French and Spanish.

16 Gretchen Bauer (2016), "'A Lot of Head Wraps': African Contributions to the Third Wave of Electoral Gender Quotas," *Politics, Groups and Identities*, 4 (2), pp. 196–213.

17 *Breaking Male Dominance in Old Democracies*, p. 248 and country chapters.

Chapter 4 Gendering Public Policy

1 Joni Lovenduski (2005), *Feminizing Politics*, Polity Press, p. 154.

2 Hanna Pitkin (1967), *The Concept of Representation*, University of California Press, pp. 114–15.

3 Cited from Shireen Hassim (2003), in Anne Marie Goetz and Shireen Hassim, *No Shortcuts to Power. African Women in Politics and Policy Making*, Zed Books, p. 81.

4 Goetz and Hassim, *No Shortcuts to Power*, p. 2.

5 Judith Butler (1990), *Gender Troubles*, Routledge, p. 3. In the 1999 edition, Butler has modified this, but her strong critique of "identity politics" became very influential.

6 See Anna G. Jónasdóttir and Kathleen B. Jones (2009), *The Political Interests of Gender Revisited*, Manchester University Press.

7 Karen Beckwith (2014), "Plotting the Path from One to the Other. Women's Interests and Political Representation," in Maria C. Escobar-Lemmon and Michelle M. Taylor-Robinson (eds), *Representation. The Case of Women*, Oxford University Press, pp. 19–40.

8 Karen Celis (2006), "Substantive representation of women: the representation of women's interests and the impact of descriptive representation in the Belgian parliament (1900–1979)," *Journal of Women, Politics & Policy*, 28 (2), pp. 85–114.

9 See Drude Dahlerup (2014), "The Critical Mass Theory in Public and Scholarly Debates," in Rosie Campbell and Sarah Childs (eds), *Deeds and Words. Gendering Politics after Joni Lovenduski*, ECPR Press, Colchester, pp. 137–63.

10 Gretchen Bauer and Manon Tremblay (eds) (2011),

Women in Executive Power. A Global Overview, Routledge.

11 Bauer and Tremblay (eds) (2011), *Women in Executive Power*.

12 Pamela Paxton and Melanie M. Hughes (2007), *Women, Politics and Power*, Pine Forge Press, Los Angeles, pp. 135–6.

13 Peter Allen (2016), "Achieving sex equality in executive appointments," *Party Politics*, 22 (5), pp. 609–19.

14 Lena Wängnerud (2009), "Women in Parliaments: Descriptive and Substantive Representation," *Annual Review of Political Science*, 21 (1), pp. 51–69.

15 See Helga Hernes (1987), *Welfare State and Woman Power: essays in state feminism*, Norwegian University Press, Oslo; Diane Sainsbury (ed.) (1999), *Gender and Welfare State Regimes*, Oxford University Press; Joni Lovenduski (2005), *State Feminism and Political Representation*, Cambridge University Press; Emanuela Lombardo, Petra Meier and Mieke Verloo (eds) (2009), *The Discursive Politics of Gender Equality*, Routledge.

16 Dorothy McBride and Amy Mazur (eds) (2010), *The Politics of State Feminism*, Temple University Press, Philadelphia.

17 Alison Woodward (2003), "Building Velvet Triangles: Gender and Informal Governance," in Thomas Christiansen and Simona Piattoni (eds), *Informal Governance in the European Union*, Edward Elgar, pp. 76–93.

18 See Amy G. Mazur (2017), "Toward the Systematic Study of Feminist Policy in Practice: An Essential

First Step," *Journal of Women, Politics & Policy*, 38 (1), pp. 64–83.

19 Mala Htun and S. Laurel Weldon (2010), "When Do Governments Promote Women's Rights? A Framework for the Comparative Analysis of Sex Equality Policy," *Perspectives on Politics*, 8 (1), pp. 207–16.

20 Theda Skocpol (1985), "Bringing the state back in: strategies of analysis in current research," in P. Evans, D. Rueschemeyer and T. Skocpol (eds), *Bringing the State Back In*, Cambridge University Press.

Chapter 5 Women in Global Politics

1 Anthony Giddens (1990), *The Consequences of Modernity*, Polity Press, p. 64.

2 Robert O'Brien et al. (2000), "The World Bank and women's movements," in *Contesting Global Governance*, Cambridge University Press, pp. 24–66.

3 Elisabeth Prügl (2015), "Neoliberalising Feminism," *New Political Economy*, 20 (4), pp. 614–31.

4 Shirin M. Rai and Georgina Waylen (eds) (2008), *Global Governance. Feminist Perspectives*, Palgrave Macmillan; Anne Sisson Runyan and V. Spike Peterson (2014), *Global Gender Issues in the New Millennium*, 4th edn, Westview Press, Boulder, CO.

5 Jofre Rocabert, Frank Schimmelfennig, Thomas Winzen and Lori Crasnic, "The Rise of International Parliamentary Institutions: Authority and Legitimation," unpublished paper, ETH Zürich, 2016.

6 Jonas Tallberg et al. (2013), *The Opening Up of*

International Organizations. Transnational Access in Global Governance, Cambridge University Press.

7 Andreas Nordang Uhre (2014), "Exploring the diversity of transnational actors in global environmental governance," *Interest Groups & Advocacy*, 3 (1), pp. 59–78.

8 Kareen Jabre (2006), "Affirmative action at the IPU," pp. 266–72 in Drude Dahlerup (ed.), *Women, Quotas and Politics*. For the most recent sanctions, see http://www.ipu.org/conf-e/135/results.pdf.

9 Louise Chappell (2010), "Gender and Judging at the International Criminal Court," *Politics & Gender*, 6 (3), pp. 484–95.

10 Aili Mari Tripp (2015), *Women and Power in Postconflict Africa*, Cambridge University Press.

11 Desirée Nilsson (2012), "Anchoring the Peace. Civil Society Actors in Peace Accords and Durable Peace," *International Interactions*, 38 (2), pp. 243–66. See also Tripp (2015), *Women and Power in Postconflict Africa*, chapter 6.

12 Aili Mari Tripp (2006), "The Evolution of Transnational Feminisms," in Myra Marx Ferree and Aili Mari Tripp (eds), *Global Feminism. Transnational Women's Activism, Organizing, and Human Rights*, New York University Press.

13 Meriam J. Anderson and Liam Swiss (2014), "Peace Accords and the Adoption of Electoral Quotas for Women in the Developing World, 1990–2006," *Politics & Gender*, 10 (1), pp. 33–61.

14 See the special issue on the implementation of SCR 1325 in *International Political Science Review*, 37 (3);

Soumita Basu and Catia Confortini, "Weakest 'P' in the 1325 Pod? Realizing Conflict Prevention through SCR 1325," *International Studies Perspectives*, 2016 18 (1), pp. 43–63.

15 Helena Stensöta, Lena Wängnerud and Richard Svensson (2014), "Gender and Corruption: The Mediating Power of Institutional Logics," *Governance*, 28 (4), pp. 475–96.

16 Rawwida Baksh and Wendy Harcourt (eds) (2015), *The Oxford Handbook of Transnational Feminist Movements*, Oxford University Press.

17 See Donatella de la Porta et al. (2006), *Globalization from below. Transnational Activists and Protest Networks*, University of Minnesota Press.

18 Ferree and Tripp (2006), *Global Feminism*.

19 Myra Marx Ferree and Christina Ewig (2013), "Global feminist organizing," in Sarah Maddison and Marian Sawer (eds), *The Women's Movement in Protest, Institutions and the Internet: Australia in Transnational Perspective*, Routledge, pp. 148–62.

20 Mina Roces and Louise Edwards (eds) (2010), *Women's Movements in Asia. Feminisms and Transnational Activism*, Routledge.

21 Sylvia Walby (2011), *The Future of Feminism*, Polity Press.

22 Gülay Caglar, Elisabeth Prügl and Susanne Zwingel (eds) (2013), *Feminist Strategies in International Governance*, Routledge, p. 2.

23 See Hilkka Pietilä and Jeanne Vickers (1990), *Making Women Matter. The Role of the United Nations*, Zed Books; Devaki Jain (2005), *Women, Development,*

and the UN. A Sixty-Year Quest for Equality and Justice, Indiana University Press.

24 P.1, see note 16.

25 As a member of the Global Civil Society Advisory Group to the Executive Director of UN Women 2012–15, first under Michelle Bachelet, later under Phumzile Mlambo-Ngcuka, I had the opportunity to follow these discussions.